TOO MUCH LIBERTY?

TOO MUCH LIBERTY?

Perspectives on Freedom and the American Dream

David J. Saari

PRAEGER

Westport, Connecticut
London

Library of Congress Cataloging-in-Publication Data

Saari, David J.
    Too much liberty? : perspectives on freedom and the American dream
  / David J. Saari.
      p. cm.
    Includes bibliographical references and indexes.
    ISBN 0–275–94879–X (hc : acid-free paper).—ISBN 0–275–94880–3
(pbk. : acid-free paper)
     1. Liberty. 2. United States—Social conditions. I. Title.
JC585.S22 1995
323.44′0973—dc20   94–22649

British Library Cataloguing in Publication Data is available.

Library of Congress Catalog Card Number: 94–22649
ISBN: 0–275–94879–X (hc)
     0–275–94880–3 (pbk.)

First published in 1995

Praeger Publishers, 88 Post Road West, Westport, CT 06881
An imprint of Greenwood Publishing Group, Inc.

Printed in the United States of America

∞™

The paper used in this book complies with the
Permanent Paper Standard issued by the National
Information Standards Organization (Z39.48–1984).

10 9 8 7 6 5 4 3 2 1

Copyright Acknowledgments

The author and publisher gratefully acknowledge permission to reprint the following
material:

Excerpts from *Man, State and Deity: Essays in Ancient History* by Victor Ehrenberg. London:
Methuen & Co., Ltd., a division of Routledge, 1974. Used by permission of Methuen & Co.

Excerpts from *The Spirit of Liberty* by Learned Hand, edited by Irving Dilliard. Copyright
©1952, 1953, Copyright ©1950, 1960 by Alfred A. Knopf, Inc. Reprinted by permission of
the publisher.

Excerpts from *Resistance, Rebellion and Death* by Albert Camus, trans., Justin O'Brien.
Copyright ©1960 by Alfred A. Knopf, Inc. Reprinted by permission of the publisher.

Excerpts from *The Ethics of Authenticity* by Charles Taylor. Cambridge, MA: Harvard
University Press, 1992. Reprinted by permission of Harvard University Press.

Translation of Pericles' *Funeral Oration* by C. W. Kalkavage, January 24, 1994.

The Human Development Report 1991 compiled by the United Nations Development
Programme. New York: Oxford University Press, 1991. Used by permission of Oxford
University Press.

In Memory of

PERICLES OF ATHENS*

Born	494 B.C.
Died	429 B.C.

Remembered for 2,458 Years

*Pericles still remains a central figure in the subject of freedom in Western Civilization. His *Funeral Oration* is in Appendix 3. During World War I, excerpts from the *Funeral Oration* were placed on the side of buses to help boost public morale. The roots of freedom and liberty are historically deep as acknowledged by this dedication. *See also* Donald Kagan's *Pericles of Athens and the Birth of Democracy* (1991), 271.

If civilization has got the better of barbarism when barbarism had the world to itself, it is too much to profess to be afraid lest barbarism, after having been fairly got under, should revive and conquer civilization. A civilization that can thus succumb to its vanquished enemy must first have become so degenerate that neither its appointed priests and teachers, nor anybody else, has the capacity or will to take the trouble to stand up for it. If this be so, the sooner such a civilization receives a notice to quit, the better.

John S. Mill, *On Liberty*, 1859

Human rights and fundamental freedoms are the birthright of all human beings; their protection and promotion are the first responsibilities of governments. The World Conference on Human Rights reaffirms the solemn commitment of all states to fulfill their obligation to promote universal respect for, and observance and protection of, all human rights and fundamental freedoms for all in accordance with the Charter of the United Nations, other instruments relating to human rights, and international law. The *universal nature* of these rights and freedoms is beyond question.

Vienna Declaration and Programme of Action, 1993

Contents

Preface   ix
Acknowledgments   xi
Introduction   xiii

CHAPTER 1. The Central Question of Freedom and Truth:
Moral Poverty or Moral Progress?   1

CHAPTER 2. Too Many Freedoms: The Evidence and
Arguments   9

CHAPTER 3. Too Few Freedoms: More Evidence and
Arguments   17

CHAPTER 4. What Is the Truth About American Freedom?
Will the Truth Set You Free?   27

CHAPTER 5. Transforming the Central Question: A Better
Perspective of Freedom, A Better Paradigm   41

CHAPTER 6. Transformed Freedom: Application of Important
Conclusions and New Beginnings for the American Dream
of Freedom   69
    Part I. National Freedom—True National Autonomy in
      a Global Society   74
    Part II. Freedom within a State or Nation: Civic Liberty   95
    Part III. Freedom from a State or Nation: Inner Liberty   106

CHAPTER 7. Transformed Freedom and the Future   117

APPENDIX 1. The Human Freedom Index and HFI Ranking
of Selected Countries   127

APPENDIX 2. Federal Preemption Statutes—1790-1991   129

APPENDIX 3. Translation of *Funeral Oration* by Pericles—
431 B.C.   133

Notes   141
Bibliography   153
Author and Proper Name Index   163
Subject Index   167

Preface

The idea of freedom is a puzzle for mankind and has been ever since people could create words to express the complex set of thoughts and feelings encompassed by the words most commonly used—freedom and liberty. It is with genuine humility that I offer a definition of liberty or freedom, knowing very well how many others have tried in the history of Western Civilization. But others were not stopped by the daunting task, so I see no reason why it should stop me from trying. This is a free country. And who knows? I may be closer to the truth about liberty or freedom than others were in their efforts. You can judge the success of that approximation to truth.

To help us think about freedom, I have constructed a framework that is based on common sense and practical experience in America and elsewhere in the past and present times. This practical approach is aimed at the widest audience possible. I have drawn on history, philosophy, law, politics, business and other fields. The definition of freedom offered is then applied to a range of significant problems in American society.

This completes the exercise except for a hope that I wish to share. The hope is that after reading this book and thinking about what I wrote, you will feel much better about asking and answering your own questions about liberty and freedom. My goal is to help you ask better questions, to continue the dialogue of freedom and liberty in your mind. It is there, in your thinking, feeling and action, that liberty thrives, changes and is reborn for every human being every day. The words written about liberty and freedom are like a mirror for reflection—to help us see ourselves more truthfully. This book may offer to you a way to unify your thinking about freedom in all of its many dimensions, and then renew your interest and faith in your own ideas about liberty and freedom.

Acknowledgments

An appreciated sabbatical leave some years ago at American University helped to launch this book. Along the way students and many colleagues pointed the way to a better understanding of liberty. Critics and readers offered help—a grateful author must recognize and appreciate this assistance as well. Attribute the best to them, the rest to me. C.W. Kalkavage's translation of Pericles' *Funeral Oration* is deeply appreciated.

A special thanks are due to Karen Woodcock and Kristin Reynolds whose technical and artistic talent made the final product appear in its best light. And one must note the enjoyment of the encouragement and warm-heartedness of Jim Dunton, the editor at Praeger.

Finally, my wife Martha's support and encouragement is the very best thing anyone could be blessed with while researching and writing. Thanks are due to her—loud and clear with love.

Introduction

In the twenty-five hundred years of recorded Western thought the authors who express diverging views about feedom are not always talking about the same thing. Sometimes they are aware of this; often they are not.

Mortimer J. Adler, *The Idea of Freedom*, Vol. 1, p. 99 (1958)

PATTERSON/ADLER DIFFERENCES

Over three and a half decades later, the observation by Mortimer Adler immediately above still is true—distressingly so. Identity of subject and clarity are central to having a rational debate. Even in so fine a work on freedom in 1991 by Orlando Patterson, *Freedom—Volume I: Freedom in the Making of Western Culture*, it is possible to echo the same belief of Adler—"Sometimes they are aware of this; often they are not." Paradoxically, Patterson began with an earnest belief that many share:

No one would deny that today freedom stands unchallenged as the supreme value of the Western World.[1]

Is it true that freedom is unchallenged by other values? Is freedom a supreme value or just one of a number of important values? Patterson said philosophers debate the nature and meaning of freedom; politicians mention it frequently; "free enterprise" business markets freedom as its own; Christians cherish being redeemed and freed by Christ; and we would die to be free. The cold war pitted two armed camps—free and unfree—against one another in a nuclear nightmare. The high value of freedom that Patterson believes to be so may be true in fact, but even Patterson acknowledged at the very beginning of his work that other values, "For most of human history, and for nearly all of the non-Western world prior to Western contact, freedom was, and for many still remains, anything but an obvious goal or desirable goal. Other values and ideals were, or are, of far greater importance to them."[2] He listed values such as glory, honor, power, nationalism, militarism, valor, filial piety, harmony, altruism, justice, equality, material progress and says the list is endless. The Western world has "inverted parochialism" in its love of freedom claimed Patterson.

Patterson asked and offered an answer to this question:

How and why did freedom emerge, develop, and become institutionalized as our civilization's preeminent ideal?[3]

Slavery was the major answer traced by Patterson across ancient Greece, the Roman Empire and the Middle Ages in Europe. Unfortunately, there was no justification offered by Patterson to assume further that freedom is modern Western Civilization's preeminent ideal or that no one would challenge freedom's position. At least not in the United States was it true that liberty was unchallenged by the multiple goals stated explicitly in the federal constitution and its many amendments. The preamble to the Constitution of the United States cites many goals including also the "blessings of liberty." The value of liberty is coordinated with other values, not superior.

Michael Kammen, a noted American historian, in *Spheres of Liberty* (1986) carefully examined over three centuries of changing perceptions of liberty in American culture. Kammen concluded that John Winthrop, James Madison and Abraham Lincoln knew, "that liberty can not be defined or appreciated as a singular quality."[4] No doctrine of liberty exists without becoming contingent on some other ideal, thus Kammen concluded that the quintessential character of liberty is its ever-changing role in American culture, not its preeminent and unchallenged place as the preeminent ideal. Kammen's evidence and analysis are sound. This finding by Kammen flatly contradicts Patterson's assertion that freedom was and is the supreme unchallenged value—preeminent in contemporary America. And, America is a part of Western Civilization. However, a real question remains: *Is liberty a contingent value and not preeminent?* That question will be explored.

As for the critical definition of the word freedom—for Patterson freedom is a tripartite value:
1. Personal freedom (not being coerced or restrained by another person),
2. Sovereignal freedom (power to act as one pleases regardless of others insofar as one can), and
3. Civic freedom (capacity of adult members of a community to participate in its life and governance).

At no point did Patterson acknowledge the existence of the two-volume study of *The Idea of Freedom* by Mortimer Adler and others, nearly 1,500 pages published in 1958 and 1961 by a group of prestigious scholars who worked from 1952-1961. There, in *The Idea of Freedom*, Adler and others examined 2,500 years of Western Civilization's writing on the subject of freedom and concluded that the historical reality of freedom is five subjects:

1. *Circumstantial Freedom of Self-Realization.* "A freedom which is possessed by any individual who, under favorable circumstances, is able to act as he wishes for his own good as he sees it." [5]
2. *Acquired Freedom of Self-Perfection.* "A freedom which is possessed only by those men who, through acquired virtue or wisdom, are able to will or live as they ought in conformity to the moral law or an ideal befitting human nature." [6]
3. *Natural Freedom of Self-Determination.* "A freedom which is possessed by all men, in virtue of a power inherent in human nature, whereby a man is able to change his own character creatively by deciding for himself what he shall do or shall become." [7]
4. *Political Liberty.* "A freedom which is possessed only by citizens who, through the right of suffrage and the right of juridicial appeal against the abuses of government, are able to participate in making positive law under which they live and to alter the political institutions of their society." [8]
5. *Collective Freedom.* "A freedom which will be possessed by humanity or the human race in the future when, through the social use of the knowledge of both natural and social necessities, men achieve the ideal mode of association that is the goal of mankind's development and are able to direct their communal life in accordance with such necessities."[9]

Each of these definitions of freedom had major historical proponents of the particular definition. One would think that writing in the liberal tradition about the intellectual development of the idea of freedom in the American Dream would include some reference, even oblique, to those contrasting, even conflicting visions of the truth of freedom's definition. This is a common characteristic of omission with unknown motivation. And that is why I start with the obvious significant definitional differences of Patterson and Adler because these definitions of freedom are like "ships passing in the night" that haunt every scholar and every other person in Western Civilization who wants to think about freedom in a serious way. The ships never see one another. When, if ever, will people in Western Civilization begin to talk and write about the SAME subject when they wish to express views about freedom? You never know.

Today there is no agreement on a definition of freedom itself. That condition is abysmal. I hope to make it plain, as a basic thesis, that a better definition of freedom could be conceived, at least better than that offered by either Patterson or Adler. The new concept of freedom is not a creature of mine, but it belongs, in fact, to Victor Ehrenberg, who suggested it in a general way in 1974 in *Man, State and Deity: Essays in Ancient History*. This superior definition of freedom is rooted in and associated here with a wide range of other viewpoints—from Michael Kammen to Walter Lippmann, Learned Hand, Albert Camus and Max Pohlenz, just to name a few. If freedom should mean anything, it ought to mean something that is the same so that we can all believe we are closer to the truth than before. There is evidence, ample enough it seems to me, to take Ehrenberg's views seriously. If we do what we have been doing, public discourse about freedom is likely to become even more incoherent than it is today.

Western thought recorded in books is recorded for one obvious reason—so that others can read it and take it into account or discount it in their thinking. This tradition of scholarship serves the truth better than any other tradition. It is simply the liberal arts tradition. I respect that tradition to such an extent that even in this introduction, I feel uncomfortable about some aspects of the written history of freedom that seem significant, but I understand less clearly than I wish to understand them. After a decade of research, I can report my conclusion that I will never live long enough to read all that has been written about freedom and liberty. My intention was to have been open to contradiction, conflict and disagreement in writing this book about the basis for thinking about freedom. Of course, readers will make their own assessment of an achievement of the goal of openness.

AMERICAN DREAM OF FREEDOM

The American Dream means a lot of different things today as it has in the past, but freedom is usually a part of the dream. Some refer to the American Dream without even referring to freedom. And I would think that having plenty of freedom plus pushing for more is normal in the American Dream. It seems that no one would object to this basic posture; I certainly do not object. Nor did my father object since he often was taken by an energizing but cryptically expressed idea—"Enough is enough, but too much is just right." William Shakespeare may be the source of the quoted expression, I do not know. And it does express the potential shade of truth so appealing in the American Dream of Freedom—enough is enough, but too much freedom is just right. This somewhat cocky idea and attitude is boisterous and troublemaking. Yet, it makes freedom an idea that has fun and games behind it, always spilling over with something new. The energizing spirit of the American Dream depends in no small part on how much freedom we will have as a people and as individuals. Too much freedom could be just right. As we shall see later in Chapter 6, Judge Learned Hand called this the spirit of "monkeying around," an inner liberty that does not interfere with other lives.

Part of the attraction of the American Dream of Freedom is its rootedness in the importance of human development to its richest potential diversity. We seem to thrive on individuality. John Stuart Mill in *On Liberty* (1859) spoke of the contrary forces of an English society and a state that made its citizens into small men mentally—dwarfing them, but "...with small men no great thing can really be accomplished." [10] The world, Mill argued, must make room for genius and other courageous original people. Such risks of liberty are worth taking to develop a better society. Eccentricity of ideas has a place in this world. Mill was quite careful in defining liberty as we shall see in later chapters. That care must account in part for the 130-year interest in his essay *On Liberty*. To this day, Mill remains a modern touchstone for thinking about liberty, although, in truth, he is located in an even older stream of thought about the idea of freedom that he acknowledged in his famous essay.

The first trouble is that a uniform definition of freedom is difficult to attain. The other contemporary troublesome side of the American Dream of Freedom is a facile or soft relativism, a narrowed and flattened individualism, a moral laxity, hedonism, narcissism, egoism and moral subjectivism that plagues America, softens individual willpower and eventually destroys an understanding of moral choice.[11] These problems go well beyond the problem of the definition of liberty, but each is an integrally related aspect to be considered in later chapters. Definition is the most important problem of the many problems to be considered, and it remains the main thread to keep in mind in the chapters that follow. What can we do to understand one another better when it comes to our mutual concern for liberty and freedom? How can public discourse improve our understanding of one another's freedom in a civil society?

PLAN OF THE BOOK

Forewarned is forearmed. The plan of the book is straightforward. Chapters 1, 2 and 3 are, or should be, troublesome material for most readers because these chapters are intended to break the quietude of your thinking about freedom and liberty in only one comfortable and personal way. Chapter 1 sketches, and I want to stress sketches, a panorama of freedom issues across America by highlighting the fierce cross-currents of ideas that swirl around us on all sides in a bewildering array of contexts. It is neither simple nor easy to understand the complex struggles for freedom in the American Dream. A significant source of confusion in the river of discourse is the exceedingly wide range of situations that involve issues of freedom. Often it seems that freedom is much like the air we breathe—it is everywhere and nowhere—unseen and powerful, all at the same time. Freedom is like the power of gravity pulling at us all of the time.

In Chapters 2 and 3 the proponents of such diverse views of freedom are stated in close-seeming opposition to one another. Obviously, I have purposely sketched both the arguments and the evidence to attempt to make stronger cases of too many freedoms in Chapter 2 and too few freedoms in Chapter 3. I do not agree completely with either perspective. But the apparent contradiction in the two chapters is even worse than contradiction—it borders on a near loss of coherence that I have tried to convey as well since the authors of such opinions do not bother to speak to one another. To an outsider such as myself, this is the way the cacophony sounds to me in public discourse. It is true babble at times. Each is going off in his or her own merry way with a line of thought or argument. Sketches of this disharmonious and disjointed public conversation is all that I can offer since neither side makes much sense to my way of thinking, but we need to keep listening to these voices to detect whatever they may offer in the way of truth about freedom.

Chapter 4 makes a final stab at finding the truth about freedom by turning to decisions of the Supreme Court of the United States and it fails in the attempt. By the end of Chapter 4 the ultimate conclusion that is reached is that all of the efforts made so far get us nowhere, and the reason for the lack of coherence lies in profound misunderstandings we suffer as a people since we do not have a common understanding of the meaning of freedom. I think a justification now is laid to try to define freedom in a more comprehensive sense in a community. Keep in mind that the first four chapters are a foundation for a single conclusion. The real challenge today lies in coming to some conclusion about the state of the definition of freedom in public discourse.

In reaction to that somber conclusion, Chapter 5 states and explains a new definition of freedom that should be tried in public discourse. To illustrate how this could be done in a contemporary application, Chapter 6 applies this new definition to a wide range of ideas, authors, conflicts and issues. Chapter 6 is one test of the vitality and practical nature of the new definition of freedom. Lastly, in Chapter 7 (as in Chapter 5) the three-sided new definition of freedom interacts contingently with other significant values--equality, authority, order, property, justice and privacy. The hope is that we can ask better questions, more thoughtfully probing questions, if we think about freedom more precisely. Contingency in liberty lies in considering conflicts with other treasured values. When "free press" fights with "fair trial" we know that absolute preeminence of freedom is an unrealistic position and belief.

Two hundred years of the "blessings of liberty" in America have enriched the American Dream of Freedom, but at the same time incoherence is haunting our public discussions. And the nightmares that haunt our body politic are with real individuals and real groups who grossly misunderstand the idea of freedom while clearly understanding whatever suits them and them alone. This is true even if the promise of freedom failed to be delivered in many cases. Sick ideas of freedom are a plague on our house, and they are an error that causes nightmares in the American Dream of Freedom.[12]

Chapter 1

The Central Question of Freedom and Truth: Moral Poverty or Moral Progress?

TOO FREE SEXUALLY AND ARTISTICALLY: ARTS, AIDS AND ABORTION

What is the condition of freedom or liberty in America today? Is it even possible to ask and answer such a basic question without a common definition of freedom and liberty? There are a number of avenues to examine, so let us begin with one of the most obvious and controversial fields of liberty.

Can we ever be too free sexually in our actions? In *The Plague* Albert Camus forces readers to think about freedom from communicable illnesses and how tenuous our hold on life really is in the face of microbial diseases such as the bubonic plague or AIDS viruses or tuberculosis that want to feed on your energy and life. Decisions to have sex help spread—communicate—the communicable disease. For the most part, people with AIDS seemed at one time to be a marginal group. Marginal people are usually an unprotected group. The views expressed show the feeling. A contemporary artist, Karen Finely, in her *Momento Mori* 1992 exhibit in the Los Angeles Museum of Contemporary Art gave an interview for the exhibit that quoted her directly:

Well, I think it's shocking that God is a white man. I find it shocking that religion is denying closure to people, denying people their identities. There's so much denial, political denial, sexual denial. There's a lot of denial in Los Angeles about Rodney King. There's a feeling that marginal people aren't worth taking care of, they're just animals. My anger comes from this.[1]

Some of us, including Finley perhaps, do care about the marginal people, even those with AIDS who may have abused their freedom.

Freer sex by conscious choice is implicated as well in the spread of AIDS. There can be no denial of this. There is some shocking denial of this action as well by gays and heterosexuals. Moral choices have deadly consequences sometimes, and AIDS has enhanced the lethal nature of choice to have sexual intercourse. No one is free today in making a choice to participate in sex to ignore the communicable disease consequences of such a choice.

Anaïs Nin, a woman writer, said, "We don't see things as they are, we see them as we are." How true that is of the subject of communicable diseases such as AIDS. We are blinded by faith in science and modern medicine, blinded by successes of modern technology and blinded by wealth and good health of Americans in general. Many think we must be impervious to AIDS viruses. To see things as they are in truth may be too painful just now, even with all of the publicity. The AIDS epidemic is a worldwide phenomena that challenges a fundamental notion that we Americans and our medical researchers, and other medical researchers elsewhere, can conquer nature, hunger and disease—no matter what is thrown at us. A Nobel Prize winner in virology in 1962 and the United States Surgeon General in 1969 saw an end at that time to infectious disease as a significant factor in social life. How utterly strange are these medical views today.

And this blindness even in the international medical community is linked to a feeling about sexuality that tumbles headlong into abortion fights in America and Ireland. These fights stir anger beneath the surface that bubbles up in the marches on Washington, DC, in confrontations and in murders in front of medical clinics that offer abortion services, and in national politics where presidential candidates and action groups argue for life, against abortion and for choice in a myriad of twisted ways that seem blinded. The president, Congress and the Supreme Court are joined in that battle as well. Do these men and a few women know reality? Who are they to want to lead a nation of 250,000,000 people? More than half of the national population is women and 45,000,000 women are in the "sexually active" category. What is the secret possession of truth the leaders hold that others do not? Can they define freedom for the people in an understandable way to promote civic harmony?

Arthur Schopenhauer in *Further Psychological Observations* stated: "Every man takes the limits of his own field of vision for the limits of the world." This statement defines some of the AIDS debate and draws us along in the need to open up our minds—especially when it comes to the meaning of freedom—freedom to have sex any way we may whimsically desire. The fear of AIDS, the fear of some types of abortions, and the fear of the uncertainty of life from womb to tomb should make us rethink our basic idea of freedom in America. Off in the distance are heard different feelings, not of rage, but of humility, gratitude, grace and peace. These feelings need a voice too, in the tumultuous world of modern urban America. It is precisely over the meaning of freedom in contemporary America that we fight so hard on so many subjects from AIDS, to abortion, to women's rights, to the Judeo-Christian heritage, to civil rights, to racial and ethnic relations in modern society, to English language-only movements—the list is long and growing. We ought to recognize a central fact finally. The polyglot diversity of the American Dream of Freedom may need to be rethought. Is it *e pluribus unum*, on the coins of America "one out of many," *or* is that vision on the coinage a dated American Dream of Freedom so now coins should read "out of many—no unity, just fights and further division?" Where in the world are we Americans headed on the subject of freedom? To stop communicable diseases we have used isolation —sanitariums—in some instances. Will we return to that strategy? And if we do, what happens to people's freedom to move about as they wish?

WOMEN, BLACKS, LATINOS, CHILDREN AND DISABLED PEOPLE

The gradual empowerment of women in politics by constitutional reordering of the right to vote a mere seventy plus years ago, since August 11, 1920, is one massive, continuous and powerful assault on male-defined realities in politics. Part of the abortion conflict results from this fallout. Just three generations of women have emerged in the United States clothed with power to vote.[2] The parallel, but much older constitutional post-Civil War (1865-1868) reordering of the value of a slave's life of being property (a chattel) into a human being's life—a citizen's life—is brimming with energy in the 1990s, as more and more black men and women are taking public office and holding high positions in education, business, arts and entertainment, sports and government. The late Justice Thurgood Marshall sat on the Supreme Court of the United States, the first black man. Governor Wilder is a first for the state of Virginia. A black, well-qualified woman was a candidate to become a southern sheriff in College Park, Georgia. The first black woman, Carol Moseley-Braun, elected to the U. S. Senate took office in 1992. Hispanic and Latino energy covers the southern United States from Miami to southern California. This change is no less than glacial in speed, but it is cutting deep valleys down the mountain sides of politics. The power is profound and dramatic—not flash in the pan or superficial. The incoming tides overwhelm the shore; the tides of freedom overwhelm the body politic in favor of women, in favor of blacks and in favor of all types of other minorities in America. A revolutionary new definition of American freedom in the American Dream is emerging from such profound clashes of human will and human determination to act and think anew as President Abraham Lincoln urged us to do. In just a few years, not decades, the American political landscape will look like nothing before in its history as the forces of political and social change alter the face of America, alter the American Dream of Freedom. Martin Luther King, Jr. energized the American Dream of Freedom for everyone. However, it is more than the "feminization" and "browning" of the American Dream of Freedom. The symbol for the license plates, ramps and parking places for the disabled is stamped now into the American psyche in such a way that it will never change back to the old insensitivities towards the blind, deaf and disabled Americans who are getting their first genuine recognition as citizens and a wider taste of freedom in the 1990s.[3] Forget pitying them; give the disabled space, new equipment, opportunities and rights is their new theme—our theme. Add women, blacks, disabled and then add youth, always knocking at the door of change and the restless rumbling spirit of America is moving forward, perhaps lurching toward a more inclusive definition of freedom now and into the next century. The "liberty for all" is certainly a universally expanding notion. The politics is one of inclusion—not exclusion—such as clubs exclusively for white males. I do not mean to belittle private clubs that are constitutionally sound associations. Privacy or exclusion is important to human development of some people as a competing value to freedom or liberty.

MENTAL ILLNESS AND FREEDOM

Think what freedom means for the mentally ill person. To avoid confinement by use of modern drugs is a paramount and humane goal of medicine. Successful treatment through drug therapy often leads to early release. But what can early release to freedom become for the mentally ill? Think of a warm 1992 summer afternoon in Seattle, Washington just before rush hour. The air is balmy, the sun is shining, the pedestrians are scurrying in their paths across steep streets and sidewalks. And there on the corner is a man with spit slobering off his lips into his beard. His disordered mind controls his body in this urbane, jet-building city on a warm afternoon above Elliot Bay in Puget Sound. The man wrenches over and his clenched fist winds up hard over his back almost breaking his arm. Why he does not fall over is beyond understanding. Over and over—the bending, wrenching and arms flying with the white spit from his mouth. The man is dressed well—his mind in shambles—a distraught man is he—immobilized on a sunny street corner while people pass by staring coldly, and then go on in stony silence. My heart sinks at such a sight driving by as I think of his release to a new form of freedom in mental illness in a public setting. Does such freedom improve the quality of his life?

Is this freedom for the mentally ill in a society that calls itself civilized? Where in the American Dream of Freedom does this man fit? Where and how will his voice be heard? He is not even *seen* by the people whose hearts seem frozen on a warm, summer afternoon in downtown Seattle. There is an agenda for the mentally ill and their personal freedom that is unfinished. Several decades ago, an academic colleague, Nicholas Kittrie of the American University Law School, began in earnest to think through the needs and rights of the mentally ill—in his book *The Right To Be Different* (1971). Here freedom and human compassion could blend into a newer code of civilized behavior, even for the man in Seattle. Human rights for the mentally ill and retarded are central to their liberty. Even taxpayers now have a statutory bill of rights in their dealing with the IRS. Taxpayers deserve liberty protected by a special bill of rights. The shift is everywhere to be seen that freedom—American freedom—is under extreme stress in many different and overlapping directions. Take the stress of illicit drugs on freedom—a splendid contemporary example.

FREE DRUG USERS AND SELLERS

There has grown to be a "drug exception" to the Fourth Amendment of the Constitution of the United States, a Bill of Rights exception to the normal requirement of a search warrant and probable cause to search and seize illicit drugs in your home, on your person, and in your car, boat, plane and cabin. "Exceptions" are the norm, getting a warrant to arrest and seize is the exception, a reversal of the intent of the Fourth Amendment that abhors general warrants and favors special warrants.

A revolution in searching and seizing drugs has been changing the meaning of freedom from government agents searching and seizing of Americans and other citizens in the United States and abroad. What exactly does this revolution seem to be? Just as British custom agents sought tea smuggled into the American colonies to avoid a British special stamp tax so too, today, do drug enforcement agents and a long list of other police officers from local, state and federal governments search and seize American citizens suspected of drug sales, possession and use. Some 20,000 agents search Americans and visitors every day—7 days a week—365 days a year, year in and year out at all times on the clock. Drug courier profiles are applied to every traveling American. Urine tests are demanded and received in a wide range of jobs—without a hint of suspiciousness or probable cause to justify them. Privacy is nil probably in autos, mobile homes, boats, planes, hotel rooms—everywhere that people are existing.

There are nuances case after case. The big-brother scrutiny is intense because never have so many been paid to search their fellow citizens constantly.

If this transformation of the meaning of freedom from arbitrary government intrusion is true, and I think it is true, then we now have reached a very practical time to consider what is meant by freedom from unreasonable searches and seizures. Every American—not just police, prosecutors and judges—has a right as a citizen to give an opinion on the meaning of the "reasonableness" of government searches and seizures. Now may be the time for a comprehensive legislative code of searches and seizures that are deemed to be reasonable in a democracy of citizens where the value of privacy is growing in importance. The legislature can check the executive branch. At least the growing Fourth Amendment interpretation that offers such an excessively broad "drug exception"—that now in retrospect seems to offer almost unlimited governmental power of intrusion —is just another example of the shape—*transformed shape*—taken by freedom from the state's power of intrusion. The third judicial branch is caving-in to the power of the sword and purse in the executive and legislative branches on searches and seizures. Who loses freedom as total collapse nears? A war on drugs is a war on privacy and a war on human freedom and liberty.

These examples illustrate the breadth of the problem in America with the American Dream of Freedom. Perhaps the problem is not with too many freedoms or too few. It may be that we truly do not understand freedom anymore, if we ever did. Freedom may have been swallowed up by a need for more authority and order, more equality and more protection of property rights. Maybe the Judeo-Christian heritage provides no protection from unreasonable searches and seizures, and that heritage should be followed to guide this nation. But is this the same Judeo-Christian heritage that includes the Spanish Inquisition of 1300-1500 and its dreadful hundreds of thousands of heretical dead in the name of God? Do Americans submit to an inquisition, too, by governmental officers so that the Fifth Amendment to the Bill of Rights, not to be a witness against yourself , is also to be disbanded in the definition of freedom in our pursuit of drugs?

As we peel away the layers of confusion and emotion, the core minimum definition of human liberty is to be found within the shell of the American Dream perhaps in its dying days. Hardly anyone could be satisfied with the definition of American freedom focused solely on criminally accused person's rights, abortion rights, women's rights, racial and other minority rights and the rights of the disabled. The rights of the white males (not an insignificant group) are just as important as any other significant subgroup in a total population. In fact, the politics of special interests thrives on creation of subgroups, but the definition of freedom in its most integrated and wholesome manner for all human beings regardless of differences requires much more thought than any subgroup has given to the broader complexities. For that reason, it would be better to suspend judgment to the end of this book. The truth about freedom in the American Dream is not reached with merely a moment's reflection. The truth is not attained by wishing it were so. The truth is attained primarily by logic and intuition, by reasoning well and thoroughly from basic premises and from knowledge of what freedom means in the American Dream. None of this is possible if one is biased toward a highly idiosyncratic perspective of freedom in America. The full evidence is conflicting about the true state of liberty in America. The definition of freedom exhibits great stress and confusion.

BASIC CONTRADICTION

These are the unanswered questions: Are there too many freedoms and human rights? Is there moral poverty or moral progress in America because of too many or too few freedoms? Is America headed for her dark ages, or for her own hell on earth? Or is America headed for a new world order of freedom wider than ever dreamed before in the history of mankind? To get at the truth, the next two chapters marshal evidence and arguments into stronger cases of too many or too few freedoms to test out what we know against a reality of powerful beliefs held by very articulate spokespersons for disparate perspectives on the condition of the American Dream of Freedom.

Chapter 2

Too Many Freedoms: The Evidence and Arguments

A BASIC VIEWPOINT

The basic argument for too much freedom for Americans goes something like this. A flawed conception of freedom— the abandonment of constraint— taking hold in the 1960s, pushed by cultural elites in universities, media, the entertainment industry and the publishing world is the source of a wide range of psychological and social disorders in America. The western idea of freedom now is promiscuity and the Englishman John Stuart Mill from 1859 on, particularly in his essay *On Liberty* gave birth to contemporary American cultural anarchy, hedonism, narcissism and general flouting of idols. Sigmund Freud was implicated as well. Mill's real progeny is license—nothing is off-limits. Moral neutrality and a fixation on individual rights is the way this perspective of liberty leads to the present chaos—a soured society is America. A soured society is "tolerant"—a ruling mantra of "new freedom." Scholars, psychotherapists and peace activists plead for tolerance when what will result is total collapse of caring about what others do to themselves. The public good has lost its meaning. It is dark, indeed, in America.

Such an advocate is William A. Donohue who said critically that there is too much freedom: "Freedom means having it all, now and forever." [1] In his book *The New Freedom* (1990), Donohue shows declining family obligations, increasing affluence and shifting risks of loss to major businesses and governmental institutions through the law, especially tort law, is the pattern of chaos. The individual has no responsibility; he has instead, just freedom, defined as absence of restraint. And he has a right to sue—lawsuit mania heading for the deepest pockets of money. A rights mania, guided by the idea of equality, is coupled with a view that "anything goes." There are no standards of excellence. This mania is found in and supported by rock music, heavy metal music, modern art and new freedom writers including Herbert Marcuse, Philip Slater and Charles Reich. The world of *Playboy*, flashy sports cars, feminists, pro-choice movements, "shacking up," no-fault divorce business and children with rights premised on equality is part of the "new freedom." The sexual revolution, pornography, the attempted legitimization of bastards, teenage promiscuity, gay rights and AIDS spreading—each of these is more evidence of too much freedom. Americans are going down the drain into the muck and filth of Swamp Despond. This is the broad sweep of Donohue's argument.

Others see irrational freedom in illegitimacy—a national bastardizing trend. Over a million divorces a year from 1975-1991, each year for seventeen years is 17,000,000 divorces at a minimum. This group is roughly a quarter to a third of the entire population. Births to unmarried women were 1,094,000 in 1989; but they were only 141,000 in 1950. That is, some 613,000 white babies and 480,000 black babies arrived in 1989. Illegitimate babies in 1989 were 27 percent of *all* births of about 4 million births. More than one quarter who arrived in 1989 were bastards. In 1950, by contrast, illegitimate babies were 3.9 percent of all births of about 3.6 million total births. What happened? What freedom was discovered in the last forty-odd, indeed, years? Over 20,000 babies a year are simply abandoned to hospitals: "boarder babies," a strange term to apply to a dreadful social condition for an abandoned orphan—a desperate fellow citizen.

As Donohue argued, the family, schools and religion were not effective because the law thwarts their role in nurturing morally responsible individuals. Liberty without limits, seen only from one person's viewpoint, without a notion of common good, coupled with endless focus on rights—this is the heart and soul of "new freedom" seen through the eyes of William A. Donohue. And he offers solutions to these problems.

ANOTHER PERSPECTIVE

From another perspective different from Donohue, one can see the argument unfolding of too much freedom in America. If we go back in American history, racial conflict tested the limits of majority rule over minority liberty in cases such as these:

- Ending of minority slavery for unwilling white majority southerners by the American Civil War
- Ending majority discrimination against blacks and others by civil rights statutes
- Ending of racial minority segregation of public schools for unwilling majority whites in northern and southern schools.

In every case there were winners and losers of freedom. Prohibition of sale and consumption of alcohol (1920 to 1933) pitted diverse interests where both sides won and lost freedom. Censorship of pornography, pariah treatment of the Mormon polygamists and the American Communist party and banning of religious practices that were out of the mainstream of acceptable religious practices, such as snake handling, peyote smoking, and animal sacrifice—all were losers. Freedom was being defined by powerful forces in American society.

More of this conflict of majority-minority interest is seen now in criminalizing drugs for recreation, the decline of criminal adultery charges, the expansion of the right to die and flouting of Sunday blue law controls. Too much freedom in America seemed to evoke an image of the extraordinary diversity of American culture, perhaps forcing some to grope for a concept of limits and of new freedoms at the same time. A mystery is generated by all of these conflicts which is difficult to resolve. Let us move on to another perspective.

Who is out-of-control and who has too much freedom in America? Take free enterprise as an example. The cast of characters is quite diverse. William Greider in *Who Will Tell The People* (1992) subtitled *The Betrayal of American Democracy* suggested that large sectors of American businesses are out of the control of the majority of the citizens. Graef Crystal found evidence that some CEOs (chief executive officers) of major corporations including the Fortune 500, paid themselves year after year, multimillion dollar annual salaries, cash bonuses and stock options plus fringe benefits even if the corporations were losing money.[2] All of this is misguided excessive freedom of enterprise. It showed vividly that the state of incorporation (Delaware for many), the shareholders, the boards of directors and the employees and unions have lost any semblance of control over CEOs. Citizen GE—General Electric—is highlighted by Greider as a corporation with real trouble about its freedom in its past, present and future. The complaints about white-collar crime and corporate corruption are part of the same evidence of a licentious savings-and-loan corporate view of too much freedom for business. It seems strange to think of some corporate CEOs and some unwed teenage girls and their lovers having the same problem, but there may be parallels since neither group seems to know much about freedom except in the sense Donohue explained—promiscuity and greed. We will return to these questions in Chapter 6. Who is out of control in the public sector?

Shadow governments such as public authorities were created often to evade bonding tax limitations of voters, while voters in 1992 and 1994 did hit a home run with term limitations of elected representatives winning in almost *every* election in states where they were put to a vote. Congress runs scared of this development. Property taxes have risen so rapidly across the nation that voters have slapped property tax limits on out-of-control public officials—from California in 1978 to Maryland in 1992. Maybe the fact that out of 200,000,000 potential, eligible voters, only half of them bothered to register to vote. In 1988, only half of those who registered did vote. But, voter apathy was misread in 1992 when larger numbers of registered voters appeared and voted. The public may be reawakening.

The arguments and evidence of millions of adults not voting, as their civic duty dictates, is a sign of abused freedom, just as gang life in major cities is such a sign; kids are out of control, armed and killing. Neither are responsible civil behaviors. Drugs are killing urban civilization and in a novelty-dominated society rappers are killing English as a language as well. Slowly, but surely, both constitutional order and limits on police action were disappearing. Law is not respected on either side, and law at the end of a gun barrel (private and public) dominated many square miles of urbanized-suburban America. Television mirrors and stimulates some of this crazy, too-free America. The norm is death to those who opposed us is morally superior to peaceful argument or discussion; this norm is a true measure of the bloody and deadly drug scene among competitors every night across the nation. Random killings on trains, in schools and in other places drive public trust into a fearful corner. In such a bloodthirsty context, the family is missing, and it is a poor teacher anyway, or too nuclear and busy to teach civility. Schools, religions and communities offered little or no guidance to young people. Car-jackings are now a federal crime; cars are now wailing little fortresses to fend off social harm. Guns are everywhere and loaded. What more evidence is needed of an odd "too free" society? Some people find these conditions of life so appalling, they do their level best to stay out of harm's way.

SOLUTIONS

Fortress America and its defensible space is already here in gated subdivisions, high walls, closed streets, bolted doors, barred windows, high-tech security alarm systems, SWAT teams, bullet-proof vests, television marketing of mace and the like. The American Dream includes a home of one's own—and it is a castle or should be a castle with moat, raised platform for entry and small holes in large stone walls for rifles. All is becoming civil war in a profound sense; there is no morality, no shame—all is or will be vulgar. The American barbarians are at work. The disordered society needs order—not more liberty. We have swapped liberty for libertinism. The argument and the evidence is striking and is frightening for many. And for many this is the reality of America that needs to be changed.

Too much freedom in America calls for more law and order, bigger prisons, and a large domestic peace corps on top of a stupendous growth of criminal justice operations from 1965 to 1993. The question is: How large must controls by public authorities become when private controls are fading rapidly? Expectations of more leveling equality based on religious belief, race, sexual proclivities, feminists rights and children's rights may now have to be toned down and lowered. The American Dream may need to expect realistically that children will *not* have a life as good as their parents. Excessive concerns for fine points of law, legal technicalities of constitutional law and justice may need to be overlooked in drug wars. Privacy may need to find an appropriately small and obscure niche in America. Government may need to be controlled so that it respects private property more fully, and alters and releases community zoning controls. Too much freedom, not enough responsibility is the theme that runs through much of America.

PARENTAL RESPONSIBILITY

Let us examine another important area of liberty. As indicated before, William Donohue laid much of the blame for the ills of contemporary America on a famous Englishman—Mill. John Stuart Mill was born in 1806 and died in 1873. He came into the world shortly after the United States became a nation under its own constitution in 1787 and had its Bill of Rights in 1791. In 1859, about the time of a free westward migration and Civil War in the United States, Mill wrote *On Liberty* in a tone that revealed an English world surrounding him and suffocating that society:

In our times, from the highest class of society down to the lowest, everyone lives as under the eye of a hostile and dreaded censorship . . . even in what people do for pleasure, conformity is the first thing thought of their human capacities are withered and starved. . . ." [3]

He said Calvinistic religious theory supported this type of human condition. And so did the Victorian Era. Queen Victoria was born in 1816 and died in 1901. Her reign lasted from 1837 to 1901; she was Empress of India from 1876 to 1901. Being prudish and observing conventions were characteristic of her reign. However, Mill probably would be startled by the United States today; it is his dream come true—rampant individualism.

Moreover, Mill carefully articulated in the hundred pages his objective of explaining a viewpoint of liberty based on a principle:

That principle is that the sole end for which mankind are warranted, individually or collectively, in interfering with the liberty of action of any of their number is self-protection. ...to prevent harm to others. ...Over himself, over his own body and mind, the individual is sovereign.[4]

Mill expressly excluded children and young persons from this principle. He said explicitly that despotism is the legitimate mode to govern barbarians—who cannot offer free and equal discussion. It was in the inward domain of consciousness, liberty of conscience, liberty of thought and feeling, freedom of opinion and sentiment on all subjects that Mill saw a need for greater freedom in his day and age. Framing one's own life and combining with those whom we wished to be with were part of this inner liberty according to Mill.

Mill expressed two maxims:

First, that the individual is not accountable to society for his actions in so far as these concern the interests of no person but himself. Secondly, that for such actions as are prejudicial to the interests of others, the individual is accountable and may be subjected either to social or legal punishment if society is of the opinion that they are or the other is requisite for its protection.[5]

How these maxims apply to a man and woman who have caused the existence of another human being by sexual intercourse and childbirth is fascinating. Mill said an intemperate or extravagant man who has a family and cannot educate or support the child should be "reprobated" and justly punished. For a man who fails to support his children, according to Mill, "it is no tyranny to force him to fulfill that obligation by compulsory labor if no other means are available." [6]

As if Mill had not exhausted his point about child support and responsibility of fathers for children's education, Mill, even in 1859, said there are "misplaced notions of liberty" that prevent moral obligations of parents from being recognized and even their legal obligations from being enforced.[7] Mill said the responsibility to bestow life may be either a curse or a blessing unless the child gets an ordinary chance of a desirable existence. Otherwise, he said, it is a crime against that child to abandon it and not educate it. He cited continental laws that prevented marriage unless parties first showed financial responsibility. He decried the then-current ideas of liberty that bent on the real infringement of the child's rights to avoid a wretched and depraved life of ignorance. It should be noted that Mill's father was a paragon of virtue in educating his son. That fatherly love obviously impressed Mill. In Mill's world there was little tolerance for deadbeat dads. This understanding of Mill makes you wonder whether Donohue ever read Mill, and if he did, whether he understood Mill's ideas.

To continue the theme of child support and parental responsibility, Donohue noted that fathers who fail to support their children are liberated right out of their responsibilities in America today. That is only partly true. Young women and their friends and families and the taxpayers and government and private charities are left holding much of the support bag of abandoned women and responsibility of child support in contemporary American society. Often, however, in reality men are left to be "stripped clean" of assets. They now join support groups of their own to mourn their loss of financial freedom. And, there may be more to come in social controls.

Governor Bill Clinton and Senator Al Gore in *Putting People First* (1992) argued about this issue the same way as Mill and Donohue. They argued for these policies:

Promote *tough child support legislation* and develop stricter, more-effective methods to enforce it: crack down on deadbeat parents by reporting them to credit agencies, so they can't borrow money for themselves when they're not taking care of their children; use the Internal Revenue Service to collect child support; start a national deadbeat databank; and make it a felony to cross state lines to avoid paying support.[8]

From 1859 to 1994, the same theme of parental responsibility and misguided liberty keeps repeating itself in England and the United States. This repetition may be a signal that misunderstanding of liberty is deeper than we think it is and more profound. But we should hardly blame a 19th century Englishman for our failings in the late 20th century. Donohue is dead wrong on the point of blaming Mill for our ills. Mill is just a dead white man to most people; a man whose arguments for liberty, as he carefully defined the term, are still valid more than a century and a quarter later. These arguments will last for another 130 years at least—to 2125.

A new "communitarian" movement in America proposes to set things right for children by dividing family assets between parents and children and at divorce setting aside some family assets for kids in their name, and by urging parents to work in child care centers, and by giving an allowance in taxes per child, and by establishing paternity at birth by putting names of both parents on birth certificates. Too much heed to rights and too little to responsibilities is a theme common to having too much freedom. A full year of family leave is proposed by this group—half paid and half unpaid.[9]

Freedom loses its meaning sometimes. The loss of meaning in a "permissive society" or in a "me generation," or in a culture of self-adoration "narcissistic" to the core, are other ways of describing America. According to Charles Taylor, the false individualism of self-fulfillment is defined in this way:

In other words, the relativism was itself an offshoot of a form of individualism, whose principle is something like this: everyone has a right to develop their own form of life, grounded on their own sense of what is really important or of value. People are called upon to be true to themselves and to seek their own self-fulfillment. What this consists of, each must, in the last instance, determine for him- or herself. No one else can or should try to dictate its content.[10]

This is an aspect of one of three societal malaises identified by Taylor. The others are an eclipse of ends and a loss of freedom. This analysis of Taylor will be taken up further in Chapter 6.

The evidence was and is everywhere that excessive freedom and misguided individuality are a significant concern and have been for some time. Too much freedom is a terrible thing in a disintegrating society—and this perspective has its ardent advocates. Somalia in 1992-1993 is such an example of too much freedom for some—true chaotic anarchy. Reduction to armed gangs and starvation of many is the result of anarchy—too much liberty.

Chapter 3

Too Few Freedoms: More Evidence and Arguments

GEOPHYSICAL FREEDOM

Nasty, brutish and short—these adjectives describe the life of mankind across the globe. Of course, these general views of the human condition are from the 1600s and are reflected in the writing of many, for example, the English philosopher Thomas Hobbes (1585-1679). Human life span was much shorter. The words—nasty, brutish and short—lay a solid geophysical foundation for the life of nonfreedom forced in the past upon the bulk of humanity. Yet recently, Somalia's starving and dying thousands of young and old are a perfect example of nasty, brutish and short human lives in 1992. Free to die of starvation is not what we think of when we think of freedom. Much of humanity on the planet is near the edge of existence. These conditions do suggest the true context within which humanity exists on a benign, but tough and demanding planet where there are few free lunches from Mother Nature and where civil war prevents normal life. Nasty, brutish, and short describes some human life even in the 20th century. There is no room to talk of human freedom and liberty in a positive way.

Space travel reinforces the blue planet's isolation in a cold, dark, terrestrial vacuum where no one is free—every human being is tethered to a life-support system of some type or enclosed in Earth-like conditions for long periods in a spacecraft. So it cannot be argued any longer from a global perspective that mankind is free to any great extent to leave planet Earth for distant planets. This is the first generation of space-capable people to face such a reality of stark geophysical earth-bound limits. *Star Trek* is just a fiction. Furthermore, the prospects of finding an Earth-like place elsewhere in the universe have grown dimmer and dimmer as space probes and telescopes have heated up the skies in the last twenty years.

Thus, a geophysical freedom for mankind over the last 20,000 years is finite—that is, within certain well-defined limits—human beings exist, flourish, die off and disappear across the globe. Whole civilizations come and go. The extraterrestrial limits of human existence are barriers that appear to be insuperable barriers—no oxygen, intense dangerous radiation from the sun, no water, no food, extreme coldness. These and other conditions place human freedom in a geophysical straitjacket made by nature even with spaceflight, commercial airlines and global positioning satellites. The essential premise, then, for those who argue that there is too little freedom for Americans is that Americans know as well as any people on earth who have explored space that there are genuine limits to human freedom that probably can never be altered. The geophysical barriers are so stupendous in nature, the probabilities of practical change in them are nearly zero.

Medical advances in America and elsewhere show human nature to be capable of extending its life—actually adding years to the bulk of humanity's life span. But once again, the design of the human body—even fed well and altered completely with every known device—is finite. The extension of life is at the end of the 20th century genuinely sensing its own limits; there is no way to prolong life. Therefore, we are not free to ignore the end of life, a geophysical property designed into the human race. There are some who think 200 years of individual life span for mankind is possible, but that is a dream time away. While we strain as a society and each person strains to keep alive, to put off the human killers—old age, heart attacks, cancer—and a long list of "other killers," it is clear that we humans are not very free at all given nature's fundamental constraints on human existence. Each decade of life in a person's journey witnesses those who fall by the wayside. The more decades of living, the shorter human life inevitably becomes to the traveler.

Both space and medical research are establishing the facts of human functions in great detail, at great expense and with minuscule advances in human freedom viewed from broad historical, philosophical and geophysical perspectives. The essential premise, then, is not that mankind has so much freedom and that a lot more can be discovered or found by scientific research. The essential premise is that mankind has interstitial freedom—little places where there is some room, but precious little, to maneuver. That is the reality as many see it for the planet and for mankind. Too few freedoms is the truth from this perspective.

Now, the paradoxical reality should not be missed by anyone. In these little niches of freedom, human beings have created gigantic intellectual worlds in Karl Popper's World III sense.[1] Even within these constraints on human liberty, mankind discovered things such as writing and poetry, symphonies, religions, electricity, air travel, computers, mathematical formulas, gravity and artificial heart valves. These discoveries illustrate that in 5,000 years of written word plus a long prelude leading to that point in time, there resulted a phenomenal abstract intellectual freedom to discover the world about us—and then to record the discovery in different ways, in pyramids in Egypt or in Albert Einstein's mass energy formula. But most important for us, mankind has discovered ways to organize himself that range from tyrannical and totalitarian orders to open, free democratic societies. Bills of rights are a discovery. Written constitutions are a discovery. Voting is a discovery. There is a lot of "prying about" by many bright minds within the niche called intellectual freedom.

The paradox of human freedom for those who believe that mankind has too little freedom is this. As the geophysical, almost absolute barriers to freedom become clearer and clearer through research, for example, in space and medicine, the piling high of human discovery and invention suggests inevitably that in World III—(the products of human imagination) it shows very little sign of limits on human freedom. And those who claim people have too little freedom focus on this intellectual plane—aware of censorship, tyranny, thought-control, torture, slavery and many ways to stifle human existence so that it is less free. The battleground scenes centered in the United States are on the Bill of Rights. Once tasting freedom, human beings seem aggressively postured to defend their freedom against small incursions, especially of their liberty from thought control by a state or a nation. Mill's viewpoint on individual sovereignty over inner liberty is widely accepted in Western Civilization.

The fears of those who see too little freedom in America are well-grounded fears based simply on the history of brutality of the 20th century. The invention of totalitarianism, defined by Hannah Arendt as one of the most devastating of political discoveries of the 20th century, is a justification for fear by itself.[2] The fear of atomic warfare brought on by war and science is no less worrisome than the fear of totalitarian regimes. Both could devastate, potentially forever for the human race, the idea of human freedom for mankind. The two inventions rank with fears of plagues, of hordes of insects descending on farmer's fields, or with fear of a resurgence of Nazi holocausts. The essential premise is that freedom is little to begin with, and it is easily crushed by human invention leading to total control in a tyrant. The resulting counter-action is simple: bend every effort to dismantle anything that threatens or may threaten human freedom, especially in critical zones such as human speech, practice of religion, association with others, international travel, and publishing of printed or other materials. These core human rights are the First Amendment, U.S. Bill of Rights, values that become the critical focus of attention and rightly so, given the logic of the human condition just spelled out above.

This then, is the opening of the arguments and evidence that Americans have too little freedom for their own good. One could argue that civil libertarians would be comfortable with the basic premise that Americans have too little freedom. It gives them a rationale for existence and a justification for an aggressive stance to defend human freedom. But the geophysical limits on human freedom have never been clearer and more reinforcing to the view of too little freedom for Americans and for others on earth. Hobbes, writing in the 17th century, was not too far off the mark long ago—nasty, brutish and short.

CIVIL LIBERTIES LOGIC

Apart from geophysical limits on freedom, and limits caused by the tyrannical societies and states formed by man, there is too little freedom if one has just a few decades to grow, develop and express one's genius of individuality. Given the shortness of human existence, is there any wonder that mankind has expressed a yearning to be free for thousands of years, especially when and where slavery was an accepted status of society. I would surmise that the cry for freedom is a constant plea that drives at least a significant part of mankind at all times, everywhere. This is particularly obvious in United Nations *Human Development Report 1991*, in which it is said: "Human development is incomplete without human freedom." [3] It is as if mankind knows implicitly what is good for its own health and survival in the long run. My guess is that where human liberty is suppressed, the yearning for it is strong. The obverse is probably true—where freedom of human beings is great, the yearning for liberty is weak, because the motivation to be free is being well fed every day, and liberty does not break out into dreams, revolutions and rebellions. This condition of great and extensive freedom (but not enough) exists in the United States today and, as a consequence, the drive for greater freedom in the United States is muted. By muted, I mean, it is focused upon apparently disconnected, specialized fields—free enterprise, abortion conflict, religious practices, police searches and seizures, death sentencing practices and the like. The muted form is cast quite often into legal disputes of a constitutional nature. Alexis de Tocqueville and others since have noticed that any major conflict in America can be cast into the form of a legal dispute that would require constitutional decision making by the United States Supreme Court. This court is the place where various aspects of human freedom have wound up being argued. The abortion conflict area is a good example. By contrast, in the last century (1800-1900) external attacks of the United States by the English in the War of 1812, the Mexican War of 1846-1848, followed by the horrific internal Civil War from 1861-1865 meant that questions of human freedom were not centered on the Bill of Rights arguments in the Supreme Court, but instead on the internal United States battlefields. By further contrast, the settling of the western United States in that century was a boon to lovers of freedom; a terror for American Indians.

Although the industrial revolution that dominated America gave a boost to free enterprise from 1870 to mass production days, beginning in 1900-20, and just about to the end of the 20th century, the real national focus in this century (1900-2000) was mostly on the external threat to American freedom during World War I (1914-1919), World War II (1941-1945), Korean War (1950-1952), Vietnam War (1965-1975), in total some twenty-two continuous major intense years of war and police actions plus the overriding Cold War (1946-1991) with a long forty-five-year evolution preceded by fears going back to 1917 and the communist revolution in the Soviet Union. The century of war placed a dramatically different stress on America regardless of its true economic development.

Issues of freedom in the 20th century that are related to security and loyalty bubbled up continuously; an example is the McCarthy Senate hearings in 1954. At the century's beginning, the pressure on liberty during World War I under the Espionage Act of 1917 and Sedition and Alien Act of 1918 made it plain, in hindsight, that too little freedom was a problem in a critical area of life—inner liberty of conscience and belief—especially for conscientious objectors to war. Inner liberty was under severe attack in the 1917 period with 2000 cases prosecuted against citizens by the United States government. Murphy stated, "Well over two thousand prosecutions occurred under the wartime Espionage and Sedition Acts. Over a thousand convictions resulted." [4] So the beginning of the 20th century presented a completely new set of threats to freedom compared with the first century of America.

Too little freedom in America is traceable to early, possibly the first, use of the words "civil liberties" in 1917 in the Civil Liberty Bureau. The civil liberties of Americans were under attack in World War I, which resulted in the creation of the American Civil Liberties Union (ACLU) in 1920. Roger Baldwin, the first executive director in 1925, started the ACLU which is today itself a critical target of attack of William A. Donohue in his *The Politics of the American Civil Liberties Union* (1985). Parenthetically, a history of civil liberties and the ACLU is now published by Samuel Walker.[5] The same William Donohue who saw too much freedom in America in his *The New Freedom* (1990) and whose viewpoint was mentioned previously in Chapter 2 continued to probe ACLU activities.

There is little doubt that the contemporary Black Freedom Struggle (1954-1990) was and is today a major internal civil rights struggle for more freedom against too little freedom. And writers like Alan Barth (1906-1979) on the *Washington Post* staff from 1943 to 1973 clearly saw this and the later years of too little freedom in his *Loyalty of Free Men* (1951) and four more books on liberty. In *The Rights of Free Men, An Essential Guide to Civil Liberties* (1983), a summation of Alan Barth's work by editor and close associate, James E. Clayton, Barth concluded that America was beginning to pay attention to loyalty and security issues but, also, it was shifting in three decades to the long forgotten issues of race, desegregation, rights of women and children and criminal justice for the poor. One way to see this better is to ask as Paul Murphy did: "Why had the politics of civil liberty *not* been a factor in shaping of public policy in the years prior to 1917? ...What was unique about national developments after April, 1917 which suddenly catapulted the civil liberties issue into the public consciousness?"[6] In other words, apart from slavery, civil liberties did not deeply concern Americans for the first 130 years of its history; why then in 1917? Why so much concern for civil liberties across the 20th century?

The answers to the questions seemed clear later to Alan Barth. Barth examined the fear of virulent anticommunism spawned by the Cold War and the era of battles over desegregation of the 1954 Brown case onward, and finally to the revolutionary era in the 1960s and 1970s in criminal law cases under decisions by the Supreme Court of the United States: *Gideon, Escobedo, Mapp, Miranda, Gault, Rochin,* and dozens more. American concern over too little freedom had a civil rights flavor, a legal flavor, a constitutional order flavor. These characteristics even mark the contemporary visions of liberty in the Bill of Rights cases.

The American Civil Liberties Union has developed a unique view of liberty. The executive director of the American Civil Liberties Union from 1978 to date is Ira Glasser who published in 1991 the book *Visions of Liberty: The Bill of Rights for All Americans.*[7] This fine book explains the ideals that lie behind many who claim there is too little freedom. It is centered on freedom of conscience and religion, freedom of expression, fundamental fairness, racial equality and an emphasis on including all Americans—gays, lesbians, abortion rights advocates and others. The essential premise of Glasser is that in America those who do not have enough liberty may often understand their own condition more clearly than untroubled others, and they, the less free, do guide the American society in a direction that leads to greater freedom for the individual and for all to follow. As a consequence, there is no single source in America for a definition of liberty. The basic premise is that these people or guides come from personal experience of a lesser freedom to wanting a greater freedom as they sense it in their lives. There is no grand design or conspiracy for people whose names made history—Rosa Parks, Clarence Gideon, Eugene V. Debs, Eugene Dennis, Jane Roe, Ernesto Miranda, Dred Scott, Homer A. Plessy and Michael Hardwick, to name a few. Too little freedom was seen in the eyes of ordinary people who did not like what they saw and felt. This ordinary citizen method is the particularly unusual and unique way that freedom in America was and is sensed most acutely. It is as if these people as citizens were the social thermometers registering a hidden heated public opinion in the minds of many Americans. They became the center of a social battle over too little freedom, a battle that was much larger than their important and individual lives.

THE ODD COMBINATION

Today an odd combination of Americans is feeling too little freedom, or so they could argue. White law-abiding adult males, wage slaves, motorcyclists not wearing helmets, smokers, people who drink liquor and then drive a car, men who sire children and want to leave the kids to others to raise, the 2,500 men (mostly) on death row (40 percent black), men who create glass ceilings for women at work, men who enjoyed the United States Navy's Tailhook Las Vegas parties, divorced men pursued for alimony and child support, Nazis and Ku Klux Klansmen, bigots of all stripes and thousands (700,000 and growing fast) in American prisons, many of whom are drug users and sellers and millions on probation and parole—these are the losers in battles over liberty who can truly claim to experience too little freedom today. The new suppressed peoples were yesterday's free men, mostly men. In a myriad of ways, technology in the form of better computers, better forensic science evidence, better communications systems and better educated police and investigators, prosecutors and judges have ended civil freedom for many. Changing social norms, successful apprehension and prosecution, and breathalyzers put an end to too much drinking and driving. Sexual harassment laws are coming down hard on males everywhere. Improved alimony and child support laws and practices are stripping clean, with computers, the wallets and bank accounts of errant fathers. And shareholders, especially institutional shareholders, are watching and checking corporate plunder by CEOs as never before. There is a downside for some less free Americans from all walks of life.

Advocates of privacy claim that there is too little freedom given the big governments as a whole, enormous government tax bureaus in thousands of political units, big police departments, a huge Federal Bureau of Investigation (FBI), enormous prisons and jails and an exceptionally large National Security Administration (NSA) and Central Intelligence Agency (CIA). A reborn set of federal regulations and sentencing guidelines may be dampening big business spirit of freedom to enjoy free enterprise without criminal responsibility. Too little freedom in the face of this big business and big governmental power is a serious social concern for any American. All of this bigness spells out trouble in the long run for a free

society. The big business of the Fortune 500 dominates the American
business world and intrudes into much of the rest of the world. The little
guy in business wonders about her or his freedom to compete in a world of
corporate giants that are getting bigger every day stretching back over the
last 100 years or more in waves of mergers. Monopoly or near monopoly
is the real name of the cartel game in world business. The wage slaves of
modern American business are worried about too little freedom in matters
such as closing down factories, shutting stores and reducing health care and
pensions. It has been a long time since America took a serious, sustained
look at income distribution and estate taxes—both designed to raise
revenues and level the rich, help the poor and satisfy the middle class.[8] Too
much freedom to make too much money is a matter of great concern to
many Americans interested in fairness of wealth distribution schemes. The
middle-class freedom is being constrained in a plutocracy evidenced by
wealthy politicians: a Ross Perot, the late Armand Hammer or a Jay
Rockefeller.

Too little freedom is sensed when people's real property figuratively
is taken by harsh zoning measures. They sense a loss of freedom when their
tax and credit records and passport files are wrongly recorded and invaded
by strangers. They sense a loss of freedom when the state can insist upon
and forcibly take blood from their insides to test for alcohol content. The
Schmerber case says no privacy can be expected in your blood stream.[9] The
middle-class question the $50,000,000-per-year salaries for any other
American, no matter how good the person. They cringe and sense a loss of
freedom when the police and network television crews break down a door
and come rushing in with weapons drawn and network cameras rolling.
They cringe even further when they see the police beating Rodney King in
Los Angeles. They ask, is this too little freedom and the answer is yes,
followed by rebellion and riots and getting even in revenge. Law and order
is itself lawless, and the government is the great, omnipresent teacher of
lawlessness and anarchy said a Justice of the Supreme Court of the United
States. Satirists have had a field day with the too free Los Angeles Police
Department over the King incident, a never-to-be-forgotten commentary on
human freedom in Los Angeles County in the late 20th century.

So now we know in broad outline the evidence and the arguments for
advocates of too few freedoms in America and advocates for too many
freedoms in America. We are tugged, each of us, in both directions at the
same time—shocked by serial killers, gang warfare in big cities and the
brutal hardening of American society in every direction. At the same time,
we fear Big Brother snooping into our private lives and some yearn for
Walden Pond. We fear big government and big business and the
regimented April 15th lock-step of taxes that the government imposes to
control people and markets. To many, Social Security has become social

seizure. The middle-class American cannot be too certain of the future of the American Dream of Freedom given the high levels of irresponsible actions by large numbers of fellow citizens who are jeopardizing everyone's liberty. Even lying to Congress has become merely a pardonable sin. Puzzlement is a normal state of public affairs given the circumstances. Puzzlement is exactly where the advocates of too many freedoms or too few freedoms leave the American public. It is hard to know what to think about liberty and freedom in America during these times.

Chapter 4

What Is the Truth About American Freedom? Will the Truth Set You Free?

BASIC ISSUE: BASIC CONTRADICTION

Beyond the issue of whether there are too many or too few freedoms in America, lies a deeper concern that comes first. Do we understand the idea of freedom well enough to know with some practical certainty that we are examining the same idea? This issue is more basic, more important and more responsive to reasoned judgment, to intuition and to logical analysis and synthesis than the particular state or condition of freedom of any society. I think many thoughtful Americans would have a difficult time accepting the idea that they do not understand freedom well. We fought wars to protect and defend it from barbarians and enemies. We all seem to agree that we are in favor of freedom. Our basic documents—the constitutions, both federal and state, and the bills of rights, both federal and state, offered enough guidance to get Americans through 200 years, and these documents still stand in daily operation and are tested in courts by reasonably well-educated people. In these circumstances, it appears likely that the truth is already known. Yet, consider the previous chapters—each giving substantial arguments and solid evidence that America is both too free and not free enough. How could such a basic contradiction continue to exist in the minds of very sincere, intelligent, and well-meaning people if something fundamental is not missing from public discourse? Contradictions of this magnitude do not exist in public discourse unless mutual understanding is somehow blocked by some sort of invisible barrier or screen. The definition of the subject of freedom is in poor condition, and that condition blocks our understanding. That reason justifies our belief that it is difficult to know what to think about liberty and freedom in America during these times.

UNITED NATIONS HUMAN DEVELOPMENT REPORT 1991

A small piece of evidence from the international research arena in the United Nations (UN) illustrates the nature of the missing factor or lack of understanding in the domestic scene in the United States. At least it offers a lesson in an openness to the basic question of the meaning of freedom that one usually does not find in writing about freedom in the United States. It echoes the statement of Mortimer Adler quoted on the opening page of this book about whether we are talking about the same thing. The United Nations work is found in the *Human Development Report 1991*. An aspect of human development is human freedom and "The Report, for the first time, includes a human freedom index. Though freedom is hard to quantify or to measure, no measure of human development can ever be complete without its inclusion." [1] An index created by Charles Humana classes Sweden in 1985 as the world's freest country with thirty-eight of a possible forty points.[2] Iraq scored zero. Most of the world's poorest nations scored ten or fewer points. Some thirty nations were in the middle. The highest scores were attained by industrialized nations including Costa Rica. Humana made clear the western lineage of United Nations human rights declarations and the corresponding difficulty that Muslims and others have in those nations that subordinate women to men or that believe in caste orders among humans or that elevate the religion over the state. Human freedom and human development move together in a positively correlated manner, the UN report concluded, because unleashing freedom sets creative energies loose leading to higher incomes and social progress. The United States came in thirteenth.

Distrust of the index of freedom was expressed immediately by the lowest rated nations wanting to *ban* the publication. William H. Draper, the program's administrator who is responsible for distribution of $1.4 billion of technical assistance aid to the third world nations, said: "We should not let our concern with finding a better way to measure freedom question the need for integrating freedom into our concept of human development. It needs no defense and it certainly needs no apology."[3]

The best defense of the United Nation's report is the objectivity of the report itself. While acknowledging difficulty in the idea of freedom, it noted further, that there existed two broad "clusters" of freedom—negative freedom from something, say arbitrary arrest, and positive freedoms called personal rights. The United Nation's report concluded that no classification system has been accepted universally—all differ in concepts, definitions and coverage. Humana distilled forty distinct criteria for judging freedom from treaties and documents that were finally selected. Even this chosen system was difficult to apply, because it remains ambiguous in what constitutes serious violations of freedom, and it provides no guidance on the relative importance of different rights. The nature of the violations is a scale disputed by some. And human freedom is a matter that may change rapidly. Lack of data makes such an index difficult to use.

Even with such difficulties, the report states in an obscure technical note an important contemporary fact about our understanding of freedom on a global basis:

Clearly, there is an urgent need for more systematic work on human freedom:
- The issue of data availability needs to be addressed;
- *The concept of human freedom needs clarification* - especially its historical and socio-cultural traditions and implications;
- and methods of measuring various human freedoms have to be designed. *We are still very much at the beginning of a systematic analysis and debate of human freedom.*" [4] (Emphasis added)

The sense of this work obviously is open to further discussion and research. The human freedom index used in the report is found in Appendix 1 of this book.

The first global meeting of great significance on human rights in the last twenty-five years was held in Vienna, Austria, on June 14-25, 1993—the World Conference on Human Rights. Representatives from 171 nations included some 7,000 participants that were supplemented by more than 800 NGOs (nongovernmental organizations). The outcome of the two-week meeting was called the Vienna Declaration and Programme of Action of the World Conference on Human Rights. The Vienna Declaration comprehensively reinforces a global belief: "The Universal nature of these rights and freedoms is beyond question" (Section I,1).[5] The Vienna Declaration spelled out thirty-nine premises for human rights, developed a plan for increased coordination on human rights within the United Nations system, recommended a High Commissioner for Human Rights and stressed themes of equality, dignity and tolerance for minorities of all kinds.[6]

However, this bit of United Nation's research evidence and Vienna Declaration in 1993 may not persuade anyone that we are just beginning a systematic analysis and debate of human freedom. Tell that to Mortimer J. Adler after his nine-year effort resulting in two volumes titled *The Idea of Freedom*. Tell that to the ACLU in its 52d year of operations in the United States. Tell that to Orlando Patterson who writes about slavery and freedom. Tell that to hundreds of writers who have examined liberty in the last 2,500 years. Tell that to thousands of lawyers in the United States who work on specific freedom issues of litigants every day. The equivalent shock would be to say to 10,000-plus researchers of the human brain that we do not know how the brain works and cannot now duplicate its extraordinary capacities. The truth is we are just beginning to understand the brain in some basic ways, the same as we are beginning to understand the deeper global meaning of freedom. The parallel is perfect. The United Nation's report is merely a hint of the true state of knowledge about freedom.

The conclusion, so far, that seems inescapable is that Americans are focused on the wrong questions and are confused, maybe hopelessly and permanently confused, about the meaning of freedom and human rights. Mill, in 1859, found England hopelessly confused about many things: inner freedom, treatment of married women, education of children and parental responsibility. His essay is quick to point out other places of hopeless confusion and lack of understanding of liberty. By opening up one's mind to the possibility of confusion, perhaps a ray of light will enter the debate arena on too many or too few freedoms. What about the nature of the debate itself?

LIMITS OF CIVIL LIBERTIES LOGIC

At this time, there cannot be a rational public debate over too many or too few freedoms because there is no agreed upon definition of freedom. How can debate be conducted when I am arguing about the lack of eggs and my debate opponent is mourning the potential loss of the *Los Angeles Times* in future bankruptcy? Two crowds assemble to shout at one another without a hint that neither is discussing the same subject. Is that, for rational people, an embarrassment, or what? One cannot construct a formal debate on too many or too few freedoms in any nation, because we do not know enough yet to do it intelligently. This may be why, in the United States, the view of a single individual, Jane Roe in *Roe v. Wade* on abortions, is the only vehicle for public discourse about women's freedom, in general, and in Roe's case, specifically, to choose an abortion. We understand one person's complaint—we cannot move the debate beyond this concrete person. Maybe the pragmatic nature of American people and American judges and lawyers operates best in this mode of concrete human concern of one person's life.

To get at the truth about human freedom may require, first and foremost, an admission of ignorance about the subject. Take a look in the mirror and who do you see? This will be difficult for some people. It did not seem to faze the United Nations' researchers just mentioned. With a more open perspective on our ignorance, we can proceed to ask about the nature of public discourse in America about freedom at the end of the 20th century. Take human slavery, does anyone advocate it? Is absence of human slavery a part of liberty and a permanent global concern? Take human torture, does anyone advocate it? Is absence of human torture part of liberty and a permanent global concern? Take the right to vote, does anyone propose eliminating it or excluding white people or people of color or women or including children? Is this right to vote a part of liberty and a permanent global concern? Take progressive income taxation, does anyone propose elimination of higher taxation of the rich to put more taxation on the poor? Is progressive taxation a valid part of liberty? Take the social, political and financial power of the Fortune 500 American business corporations as an example of liberty, does anyone propose total governmental seizure and take-over of the Fortune 500? Not even Ralph Nader argues for such a proposition to free America, although federal chartering of giant corporations from President James Madison to Nader has had its advocates. Is this part of liberty? Finally, take the Bill of Rights, does anyone propose their swift and complete elimination? Is this part of liberty?

In many ways, these rhetorical questions sharpen the debate about liberty, and they reinforce one truth—constitutional order evolved over the last 200 years in the United States fairly well expresses the meaning of democracy and freedom. But the truth also suggests that the constitutional order, articulated so well by Ira Glasser's *Visions of Liberty*, is not the sole means of understanding American freedom or freedom elsewhere. It is true that the Bill of Rights perspective is one of great, pragmatic and political power in the United States. But it is not the sole avenue of defining freedom. For example, there are separation of powers considerations that affect freedom as well. For some lawyers and ACLU advocates, the proposition that the Bill of Rights is part of the story will be very difficult to accept as truth. Just how difficult this acceptance will be can be seen in the highest level of debate about liberty in the Supreme Court of the United States in recent years. If any place has examined liberty carefully, it was the Supreme Court in what are called civil liberties cases. For this reason, and because of the recent nature of discourses there on liberty, we should examine how truth about liberty is approached by the United States Supreme Court in the decision *Planned Parenthood of Southeastern Pennsylvania v. Robert R. Casey* decided June 29, 1992. I would classify this case as a civil liberties case. It is now an important decision about the meaning of liberty in America.

PLANNED PARENTHOOD OF SOUTHEASTERN PENNSYLVANIA V. CASEY AND LIBERTY

While reaffirming the basic idea of *Roe v. Wade* (1973) that a woman has a right to privacy early in pregnancy, the Supreme Court upheld all of a restrictive Pennsylvania statute on abortion except for declaring unconstitutional a provision requiring a woman to notify her husband of the abortion before obtaining one. In other words, the highest federal court told one of the fifty state legislatures and one of the 50 state governors that they were wrong to pass and to try to enforce such state positive law statutes enacted by a majority in a male-dominated state legislature and attempted to be enforced by a white, male governor named Robert P. Casey who clearly wants abortion rights of Pennsylvania women restricted by statutory rule. The five abortion clinics, a physician and a class of doctors who brought action against the State of Pennsylvania sought a declaratory judgment that each of the state statutes was unconstitutional on its face. The Federal District Court struck down all of the statutes as unconstitutional and permanently enjoined enforcement by Governor Casey. On appeal, the Federal Court of Appeals struck the husband notification statute but upheld the rest of the state statute, which led to the appellate decision by the United States Supreme Court. The result was that powerful regulations of abortion in statutory form do now control abortion in Pennsylvania. Some view this as a total collapse of *Roe v. Wade* and are pessimistic. Included are informed consent provisions, parental consent provisions, abortion facility controls, publication of abortion literature by the state, and reporting requirements by physicians and facilities. But, the emerging definition of liberty should offset some of the pessimism because it is a reaffirmation and clarification of the idea of freedom in abortion conflicts.

It is important to see firsthand what the Supreme Court struck down in the state law—the spousal notice provision. The following is section 3209 Spousal Notice of the 18 Pennsylvania Consolidated Stat. Ann. (1990) from Selected Provisions of the 1988 and 1989 Amendments to the Pennsylvania Abortion Control Act of 1982:

§ 3209. Spousal Notice.

a. Spousal notice required—In order to further the Commonwealth's interest in promoting the integrity of the marital relationship and to protect a spouse's interest in having children within marriage and in protecting the prenatal life of that spouse's child, no physician shall perform an abortion on a married woman, except as provided in subsections (b) and (c), unless he or she has received a signed statement, which need not be notarized, from the woman upon whom the abortion is to be performed, that she has notified her spouse that she is about to undergo an abortion. The statement shall bear a notice that any false statement made therein is punishable by law.

b. Exceptions—The statement certifying that the notice required by subsection (a) has been given need not be furnished where the woman provides the physician a signed statement certifying at least one of the following:

    1. Her spouse is not the father of the child.

    2. Her spouse, after diligent effort, could not be located.

3. The pregnancy is a result of spousal sexual assault as described in section 3128 (relating to spousal sexual assault), which has been reported to a law enforcement agency having the requisite jurisdiction.

4. The woman has reason to believe that the furnishing of notice to her spouse is likely to result in the infliction of bodily injury upon her by her spouse or by another individual.

Such statement need not be notarized, but shall bear a notice that any false statements made therein are punishable by law.

c. Medical emergency—The requirements of subsection (a) shall not apply in case of a medical emergency.

d. Forms—The department shall cause to be published, forms which may be utilized for purposes of providing the signed statements required by subsections (a) and (b). The department shall distribute an adequate supply of such forms to all abortion facilities in this Commonwealth.

e. Penalty; civil action—Any physician who violates the provisions of this section is guilty of "unprofessional conduct," and his or her license for the practice of medicine and surgery shall be subject to suspension or revocation in accordance with procedures provided under the act of October 5, 1978 (P.L. 1109, No. 261), known as the Osteopathic Medical Practice Act, the act of December 20, 1985 (P.L. 457, No. 112), known as the Medical Practice Act of 1985, or their successor acts. In addition, any physician who knowingly violates the provisions of this section shall be civilly liable to the spouse who is the father of the aborted child for any damages caused thereby and for punitive damages in the amount of $5,000, and the court shall award a prevailing plaintiff a reasonable attorney fee as part of costs.

This state law of Pennsylvania is extraordinarily clear and powerful in its message to the medical profession. It says that if you violate this law you can be kicked out of the medical profession, and you can be "civilly liable" to the spouse who is the father of the aborted fetus for any damages and for $5,000 in punitive damages. And, if the physician loses, he pays the winner's "reasonable attorney fees" as part of the costs. To follow this precise part of the *Casey* decision, it is important to notice what the majority of the Supreme Court said about such a spousal notification statute:

Section 3209 embodies a view of marriage consonant with the common-law status of married women but repugnant to our present understanding of marriage and of the rights secured by the constitution. Women do not lose their constitutionally protected liberty when they marry. The constitution protects all individuals, male or female, married or unmarried, from abuse of governmental power, even where that power is employed for the supposed benefit of a member of the individual's family. These considerations confirm our conclusion that Section 3209 is invalid.

The Supreme Court reviewed the spousal notice law carefully by examining the record of numerous expert witnesses and the detailed findings of the district court which numbered at least 298 findings. The court reviewed findings by the American Medical Association on domestic violence. Many other studies on domestic violence were reviewed. The court noted one study that found women usually notify husbands of pregnancy except for those that are the result of extramarital affairs where such a notice may cause reasonable fear of abuse in women. The common-law and prior court decisions on abortion were reviewed, all leading to the ultimate conclusion: "A state may not give a man the kind of dominion over his wife that parents exercise over children." In other words, a married woman is not her husband's child in modern constitutional law. This may continue to shock some men.

The Supreme Court rejected the old common law view of married people by stating: "These views, of course, are no longer consistent with our understanding of the family, the individual, or the Constitution." This then, is the basic Court decision; but for our purposes, it is important to focus further upon the reasoning of the Supreme Court majority opinion with regard to the meaning of liberty in this type of broad, public-policy case.

The majority begins with an "august and sonorous" statement: "Liberty finds no refuge in a jurisprudence of doubt." The Court finds constitutional protection for a woman's decision to terminate her pregnancy from the Due Process Clause of the Fourteenth Amendment of the United States Constitution passed in 1868, that declares that no state shall "deprive any person of life, liberty, or property, without due process of law." The controlling word is "liberty—a substantive right. The Court says: "It is a promise of the Constitution that there is a realm of personal liberty which the government may not enter." The realm of personal liberty includes decisions of who to marry, whether to use contraceptive devices, and how to educate your children. The Court said that by 1973 in the *Roe v. Wade* decision it was settled law that the Constitution places limits on a state's right to interfere with a person's most basic decision about family and parenthood. The Court recognized the balance that must be struck between individual liberty and the demands of organized society, and it paid respect to the disagreements people have over terminating pregnancies. But it said, "Our obligation is to define the liberty of all, not to mandate our own moral code."

Most significantly the Court wrote, "The underlying constitutional issue is whether the state can resolve these philosophic questions in such a definitive way that a woman lacks all choice in the matter, except perhaps in those rare circumstances in which the pregnancy is itself a danger to her own life or health, or is the result of rape or incest." The Court reference is to the spousal notification statute that provides a "definitive way" for women to act—perhaps not in their best interests—to notify a husband that he is not the father of his wife's pregnancy. What follows after the notice may not concern the state, but it does concern the woman and her husband.

Finally, the Court got down to the crux of the meaning of liberty. The following quotation from the opinion is rather long, but it is the current basis of defining liberty in the United States, where all governments can be kept out of the private realm of personal liberty in marriage, procreation, contraception, family relationships, child rearing and education:

Our law affords constitutional protection to personal decisions relating to marriage, procreation, contraception, family relationships, child rearing, and education. *Carey v. Population Services International*, 431 U.S., at 685. Our cases recognize "the right of the *individual*, married or single, to be free from unwarranted governmental intrusion into matters so fundamentally affecting a person as the decision whether to bear or beget a child." *Eisenstadt v. Baird, supra*, at 453 (emphasis in original). Our precedents "have respected the private realm of family life which the state cannot enter." *Prince v. Massachusetts*, 321 U.S. 158, 166 (1944). These matters, involving the most intimate and personal choices a person may make in a lifetime, choices central to personal dignity and autonomy, are central to the liberty protected by the Fourteenth Amendment. At the heart of liberty is the right to define one's own concept of existence, of meaning, of the universe, and of the mystery of human life. Beliefs about these matters could not define the attributes of personhood were they formed under compulsion of the State.

These considerations begin our analysis of the woman's interest in terminating her pregnancy but cannot end it, for this reason: though the abortion decision may originate within the zone of conscience and belief, it is more than a philosophic exercise. Abortion is a unique act. It is an act fraught with consequences for others; for the woman who must live with the implications of her decision; for the persons who perform and assist in the procedure; for the spouse, family, and society which must confront the knowledge that these procedures exist, procedures some deem nothing short of an act of violence against innocent human life; and depending on one's beliefs, for the life or potential life that is aborted. Though abortion is conduct, it does not follow that the State is entitled to proscribe it in all instances. That is because the liberty of the woman is at stake in a sense unique to the human condition and so unique to the law. The mother who carries a child to full term is subject to anxieties, to physical constraints, to pain that only she must bear. That these sacrifices have from the beginning of the human race been endured by woman with a pride that ennobles her in the eyes of others and gives to the infant a bond of love cannot alone be grounds for the State to insist she make the sacrifice. Her suffering is too intimate and personal for the State to insist, without more, upon its own vision of the woman's role, however dominant that vision has been in the course of our history and our culture. The destiny of the woman must be shaped to a large extent on her own conception of her spiritual imperatives and her place in society.

The quotation immediately above is the most extensive definition of personal inner liberty that has been attempted by the Supreme Court to date. Evidence of the extensive nature is when the Supreme Court writes, "At the heart of liberty is the right to define one's own concept of existence, of meaning, of the universe, and of the mystery of life. Beliefs about these matters could not define the attributes of personhood were they formed under compulsion from the state."

In other words, the state ought not try to define the religious nature of the abortion decision for women, since their religious beliefs are their inner private views. Even more profoundly the Court noted that the zone of conscience and belief is philosophical, but abortion is an act as well. The Court examined the unusual liberty of a woman to terminate pregnancy—unique to the human condition and unique to the law. The Court said no matter what the dominant vision has been in the course of American history and American culture, "The destiny of the woman must be shaped to a large extent on her own conception of her spiritual imperatives and her place in society." These are powerful words!

This is not unlike John Stuart Mill who, in 1859, severely criticized, "The almost despotic power of husbands over wives . . . wives should have the same rights and receive the protection of the law in same manner as all other persons. "[7] Here again, it is significant to note that the same English common law that allowed husbands to lord over wives in 1859 during Mill's time in England is struck down in 1992 in the United States by explicit rejection of the notion of the common law domination and associated false superiority of the male in the marriage. No doubt, Mill would be smiling from Heaven, if he could read the *Casey* decision, saying to himself: "See, I told you the English society, culture and common law were outrageous and stifling 133 years ago, and on some issues, now you can see how awful it can be as it spreads overseas to America and its legislatures dominated by unthinking men." What majority with what vision is speaking in modern legislatures? In late 1992 data, the Washington state legislature was 38 percent women, the Pennsylvania legislature 9.9 percent women.

The dissents of the Justices in the *Casey* opinion state, for the most part, conclusions and poke fun at "anything so exalted as my views concerning the concept of existence, of meaning, of the universe, and of the mystery of life." The dissent ridicules the jurisprudential concerns of the majority that are viewed as Orwellian.

Oddly, one Justice in dissent concludes, "We should get out of this area, where we have no right to be, and where we do neither ourselves nor the country any good by remaining." This is a superb response that pregnant women may appreciate from so high an official. A response to this concern is that it is easy to disqualify one's self in judging a case because of the lack of impartiality, and furthermore, there are solutions to removing one's self that are even more characteristically personal, including resignation from the Supreme Court, which any Justice is free to do. If the going is too tough, one can always leave the scene. This form of escapism by dissent from the reality of decision making is itself a choice to continue self-torture over issues one is perhaps loathe to decide. But, it is possible that the intense degree of dissenter discomfort is saddled with an honest assessment of personal ignorance about the meaning of freedom. In this, none of the Justices would be alone. All would face a mystery of life as profound as descending 35,000 feet to the bottom of the Marianas trench in the Pacific Ocean or ascending to the moon and walking on it. There are intellectual mysteries in the sea and on the moon and, also, before our eyes in matters most mundane, but genuinely wonderful, including human freedom.

I would give the Supreme Court majority in *Casey* praise for creating more certainty in jurisprudential matters that touch upon the meaning of liberty in the American society. Furthermore, citizens of the democracy—preoccupied as they are with their own lives—do not have time, opportunity or inclination to explore the more profound meaning of liberty as it is evolving in the American society today. Thus, the praise here is sincere, but the *Casey* decision still is not made within a larger, coherent framework of the meaning of liberty over the last 2,500 years, nor is the meaning of liberty sensitive to the wide range of other meanings it has outside the context of the opinion on abortion. The UN material mentioned previously is part of the wider context, for example. For this reason, a jurisprudential concern for the meaning of liberty would be helped by broader perspectives on other topics different from abortion. The narrowness of the meaning of liberty is the principal characteristic of the *Casey* decision made by the majority. In contrast, the dissenters appear to be narrow-minded when it comes to the intellectual responsibility to define and argue about liberty, because they did not responsibly join issue with the majority and debate the meaning of liberty in either a jurisprudential or constitutional sense or in any other sense. That failing is quite serious for the American body politic that has every right to expect more of the dissenters both as public officials and as fellow citizens. This field is, after all, the very heart of defining constitutional order for 250,000,000 fellow citizens, and judicial ethics demand that it be taken seriously by judicial incumbents as an intellectual and traditional heritage of the Supreme Court of the United States. Public institutions and their incumbent officials have many subjects to consider and this may account, in part, for intellectual deadness in the dissenters on the meaning of liberty.

SEARCHING FOR TRUTH

The question of the meaning of liberty even for the Supreme Court becomes one of a search for truth. In this search, what other avenues could be explored to understand freedom in America more precisely? The basic alternatives are history and philosophy. Essentially, we need a definition of human freedom that exceeds in scope that of the American Constitution and the Bill of Rights. We need a definition more complete than what journalism, law and social science can provide now, one which looks beyond the territorial and intellectual space of the United States. The universal meaning of freedom as accepted by the United Nations seems to be appropriate. Locating freedom in Western Civilization much as Mortimer Adler and Orlando Patterson have attempted is the most productive and illuminating direction to take in the future.

We can escape from the strict focus on the Bill of Rights by remembering the experimental nature of the United States Constitution. Redefining the nature of freedom can be done within the Constitution and Bill of Rights, and it can be done outside the Constitution and the Bill of Rights. Both are important ways to approach the truth, neither of which is exclusive. Civil libertarians often forget this truth about the limits to civil liberty logic which focuses on the Bill of Rights exclusively.

The search for truth must take into account the decline of interest in a balanced federalism and a separation of powers vitality as basic ways to organize a life of greater freedom in a society. It is easy to agree with Charles Taylor, who sees America fragmenting itself with too intense governance through Supreme Court decisions at the national level as illustrated by *Roe v. Wade* and the *Casey* decision. Being able to form a common purpose and carry it out—the will to govern in the majority—is hedged with extraordinary constraints and is unbalanced or lopsided according to Taylor. Excessively fragmented societies find it difficult to carry out majority tasks as a community, so we must consider this further in the next chapter and the last chapter. According to noted civil libertarian and academician Henry Steele Commanger we have solved the problem of national supremacy, and we should not allow commitment to the principle of separation of power or to the "anachronism" that "that government is best which governs least" to stop the Supreme Court from its obligation to find justice—all of this sounds more than a bit flat and hollow today. This is a troublesome narrowing of the meaning of freedom for a liberal scholar to the confines of whatever a current majority of a court may pronounce.[8]

Without a vibrant broad vision of liberty and freedom to energize the American Dream, and a vision that provides a unifying theme for the body politic on July Fourth and other times of the year and on great occasions—there is not a feeling of loyalty, a feeling of belonging to something larger, a feeling of community that is supportive, not suppressive. A freedom based upon morality broadly conceived and where what is right and what is wrong is shared widely, is a freedom that makes sense way beyond a bare majority passing a statute or ordinance. A freedom to cause trouble that is not criminal in nature is a noble freedom. A vision of liberty that has artistic energy driving its soul is a vision that would carry a large modern democracy far into the future. The heartbeat of the American Dream of Freedom must have more to do with a love of freedom honestly understood (warts and all) than a love of driving automobiles and the commercialized freedom that may be falsely inspired especially on clogged freeways. Martin Luther King, Jr. put us on the right track to truth. The truth about the American Dream of Freedom is not clear, not well understood, and not accepted widely in the society. This is true for the august Supreme Court of the United States as well as for the ordinary citizen. My guess is that the truth has not yet set America free to rise to the heights of civility to which it could aspire and should aspire in human freedoms and human rights.

Chapter 5

Transforming the Central Question: A Better Perspective of Freedom, A Better Paradigm

JUSTIFYING TRANSFORMATION

The aim of this chapter is to set forth a better definition of freedom and, in so doing, transform the old debate about too many or too few freedoms into a new paradigm of liberty based on a new definition. By better definition, I mean one that is more comprehensive and clear than that offered by both noncivil and civil libertarians, but it will include both of their views. By better definition, I mean to be comprehensive by being responsive to both the recent United Nations research of its freedom index and to the *Oxford English Dictionary* as well as definitions offered by Isaiah Berlin, Immanuel Kant, Mortimer Adler, and many others who are leading expositors on the subject of freedom in Western Civilization.

The justification for the transformation of freedom is quite obvious. In previous chapters, there is little question that the polarities of argument that Americans are too free or not free enough are unresolvable conflicts of opinion without refined analysis of just what aspect of liberty is being examined in each argument and precisely where the disagreement lies. These types of analyses get nowhere, and they lead to public confusion. Incoherence is the result.

An important exclusion is made here. John Stuart Mill began *On Liberty* by carefully omitting any discussion or analysis of the issue of free will versus determinism, since his focus was on the extent of state authority over an individual's inner liberty. The definition proposed here omits the indeterminism and human freedom issue: Is man a free agent? I agree in general with Karl Popper's analysis that physical determinism is a nightmare.[1] I omit this subject of "free will versus determinism" because it would take us too far from the direction I wish to take you.

A better definition of liberty is, or should be, easily understood in the English language with a minimum of obscurity or ambiguity. The minimum ambiguity that must be tolerated by one and all is the ambiguity of the language itself that neither I, nor any other person, can eliminate completely. This is a reality that should be accepted as an inevitable concomitant of the use of human language. But we can learn a lot more about the sources of confusion and ambiguity that we will get to shortly.

A better definition of liberty is, or should be, a potential springboard to even better definitions in the future. These future better definitions are the responsibility of others. I have always admired the scientific spirit in this regard when it urges us to form hypotheses about the world, then accept them provisionally, even try to falsify them, but always keeping an open mind of the truth in its ultimate sense of certainty while we act on what we know now. The task ahead lies beyond any known method of science, thus we must depend on other fields of knowledge, principally history, philosophy and law.

DEFINING LIBERTY: DIFFERENT APPROACHES

Forty aspects of freedom are listed in Charles Humana's *World Human Rights Guide* (1986). They range from the personal right to determine the number of one's children (an obvious negative reflection on Chinese birth control policies) to the freedom from torture or coercion. All of the forty aspects are basic human rights, or so it seems. By contrast, in a widely discussed definition of liberty, Isaiah Berlin in *Four Essays on Liberty* (1969) defined liberty (although he said there existed more than 200 senses of this protean word) in a simple bifurcation—a negative sense of liberty and a positive sense of liberty. The negative sense of liberty responds to this question: "What is the area within which the subject—a person or group of persons—is or should be left to do or be what he is able to do or be without interference by other persons?" [2] The positive sense of liberty is "What, or who, is the source of control or interference that can determine someone to do, or be, this rather than that?" [3] One approach, that of Humana, is an expanding definition; the other, by Berlin is a parsimonious and probing approach.

A UNITED NATIONS APPROACH

One key to developing a general definition of freedom is found in the *UN Human Development Report 1991*. It is the study that I found previously to have a remarkably open attitude towards the tasks of defining liberty.

"Let's work on it" is the attitude from a global perspective. The 1993 Vienna Declaration is one outgrowth from such an attitude. Previously, in Chapter 4, I referred to this attitude of objectivity. There is a dramatic difference between those who have closed their minds about the meaning of freedom and human rights compared with those persons who are still open to definitional alternatives and options. My guess is that there will be no closure of the definition of liberty in the 20th century, perhaps even in the 21st century. It is not the purpose of this book to bring closure to the subject. It may be that a final definition of freedom will forever elude mankind's grasp, just as immortality and the Fountain of Youth have escaped the grasp. But the tasks are so important; the time it takes is worth the effort. Imagine the centuries it took to build Christian cathedrals in Europe, evidence of the intergenerational creative spirit. What I am trying to say is that freedom and liberty and human rights need a universal definition so that no one on the globe could claim to have a superior and different and possibly conflicting definition. The goal is to see that the definition of freedom is parallel to the law of gravity by analogy—a universal phenomena.

THE PRESIDENT LINCOLN APPROACH

If any president of the United States needed a definition of liberty it was Abraham Lincoln (1809-1865). He is the president who dealt with the bondage of slavery, disunion, civil war (1861-1865) and reconstruction. At a public fair in Baltimore, Maryland, on April 18, 1864, he said a widely quoted statement:

The world has never had a sound definition of the word liberty, and the American people, just now, are much in want of one. We all declare for liberty; but in using the same *word* we do not all mean the same *thing*. With some liberty may mean for each man to do as he pleases with himself, and the product of his labor; while with others the same word may mean for some men, to do as they please with other men, and the product of other mens' labor. Here are two, not only different, but incompatible things, called by the same name—liberty. And it follows that each of the things is, by the respective parties, called by two different and incompatible names—liberty and tyranny.[4]

One hundred and twenty-seven years later in *The Fate of Liberty* (1991) Charles E. Neely, Jr. could state unequivocally about Lincoln and the American Civil War: "War and its effect on civil liberties remain a frightening unknown."[5] I wonder. The first suspension of the writ of habeas corpus by President Lincoln on May 10, 1861 was directed to Florida that seceded from the Union. By September 24, 1862, the writ was suspended by Lincoln throughout the nation in certain kinds of cases. Over a century later, historians are still attempting to ascertain the meaning of about 14,000 arrests made during the Civil War that could have been challenged in court by a writ of habeas corpus. Neely found many of the arrests associated with conscription rather than arrests to stifle dissent of government war policies. But the record is far from clear.

Abraham Lincoln is the same person fighting for an end to slavery and to protect the union of states that, also, during rebellion challenged freedom of fellow citizens by suspension of the writ of habeas corpus. Just before he was assassinated, Lincoln said a good definition of liberty is needed by the American people. However, lack of definition did not prevent the Civil War.

DICTIONARIES, USAGE AND HISTORY

Western usage of the words *liberty* and *freedom* reveals some fascinating characteristics in English and American practices as recorded in dictionaries of a general nature. These may be helpful.

1. *Freedom* and the word *free* are developing more meanings than is *liberty*. Tracing the *Oxford English Dictionary* from 1933 to 1989, the fifty-six-year growth of the meanings of *freedom* and *free* far outstrips those for *liberty*.
2. *Freedom* and *liberty* are used interchangeably by some knowledgeable authors.
3. *Free* in the 1989 *Oxford English Dictionary* is the most extensively defined word compared with *freedom* and *liberty*. The word *free* has four major distinctions:
    Not in bondage to another
    Released, loose, unrestricted
    Characterized by spontaneity, readiness or profuseness in action
    Not burdened, not subject or liable, exempt, invested with
       special rights or privileges.
    Some thirty-two separate definitions are located within these four broad categories.
4. *Freedom* in the 1989 *Oxford English Dictionary* has fifteen distinct definitions. The word *liberty* has nine distinct definitions in the same publication.
5. In general usage, *free* in its primary first meaning is defined as not in bondage to another, not bound or subject as a slave to his master. *Liberty* is primarily exemption or release from captivity, bondage, or slavery. Both terms stress that physical confinement or restriction, for

example, by force is antithetical to the meaning of free or liberty. The idea of slavery is central to understanding freedom and liberty even today in the 1989 *Oxford English Dictionary* no matter how many other nuances follow on the meaning of the words.

The legal use of the words *liberty* and *freedom* follow some of the same characteristics of general dictionaries. These are:

1. While *Black's Law Dictionary* (abridged 6th edition, 1991) and the *Oxford Companion to Law* (1980) both find widespread use of *liberty* and *freedom*, the legal usage in the United States is expanding for both *liberty* and *freedom*, while English usage clearly is expanding for the word *freedom*, not *liberty*.

2. Legal usage ties both *liberty* and *freedom* to significant legal concepts found in constitutions, statutes and common law. In the United States, freedom of association, freedom of choice, freedom of contract, freedom of expression, freedom of press, freedom of religion, freedom of speech and the Freedom of Information Act, a statute, are major subjects. *Liberty* includes civil liberty, liberty interest, personal liberty and political liberty. All are significant topics. In England, the idea of *freedom* includes academic freedom, intellectual freedom, political freedom, freedom from arrest or molestation, freedom from discrimination, freedom of access, freedom of assembly, freedom of association, freedom of belief and opinion, freedom of communication, freedom of conscience, freedom of contract, freedom of expression, freedom of religion, freedom of speech and expression, freedom of the press, freedom of the seas, freedom to hold private property, freedom to work—some nineteen different properties exist in the idea of freedom in English law.

3. The links between common use of the words *liberty* and *freedom* and legal use of the same terms are very important for thinking about the translation of an abstract right into a concrete reality to be enjoyed by a specific human being in a definite time frame. The case of *Roe v. Wade* illustrates this well; so does the *Gideon* decision on the right to counsel for poor people.

C. S. Lewis in *Studies in Words* (1967) said "verbicide" is the murder of a word by inflation, by verbiage, by snatching a word for its selling quality and by loss of a descriptive quality—loading a word down with evaluative qualities.[6] Lewis acknowledged (1) that words constantly take on new meanings; (2) that words in their context have definite meanings; (3) that words are associated with historical circumstances (such as Lincoln's speech on liberty); and (4) other observations too numerous to summarize here. Lewis analyzed the word free in a way that may help to open a skeptic's mind.[7] That is why I wish to dwell on his approach, perhaps to break the spell of old meanings.

Lewis focused upon the word *free* in its Greek, Latin and Frank roots. Both the Greek root *eleutheros* and the Latin root *liber* are used to describe a free person. The Frank root is different and is related to Frank conquerors of Gaul and their being *free* as opposed to being in the unfree state of serfs attached to the Roman villa; such an unfree person was a *villanus* or *villain*. Each of these roots of the word *free* has a different character that Lewis identified as follows.

The Greek root of free occasionally referred to slaves who Lewis says are not ordinary meek slaves. By way of contrast, "The true servile character [of a Greek slave] is cheeky, shrewd, cunning, up to every trick, always with an eye to the main chance, determined 'to look after number one.'" [8] These more aggressive slaves always had an ax to grind. Greek and Roman comedy portrayed them this way according to Lewis.

The Latin root *liberalis* related to liberality. Cicero is quoted as saying, "Liberales are the sort of people who ransom prisoners of war." [9]

While Greek and Latin roots of free refer to legal status, the word *free* in Anglo-saxon roots such as *freora manna*, referred to sons of freemen who would be taught to read according to King Alfred's usage. Literacy is linked to freedom.

Lewis observed that the word *free* in English is feudal in background where manners also became significant, compared with the Greek and Roman state-related meanings. The words of Chaucer associated the ideas truth, honor, freedom and courtesy—all showing "highest self-sacrifice and manners down to the smallest gracefulness in etiquette." [10] The words *free* and *frank* remain straightforward and bold of a noble nature.

In what is characterized by Lewis as an "obsolete branch line" —*eleutheria* and *libertas* or freed and franchise—could refer to the legal freedom of an entire community. Today these words refer to the freedom of a state. To quote Lewis:

The contrast implied is sometimes between autonomy and subjection to a foreign power; sometimes between the freedom of a republic and the rule of a despot. The medieval words nearly always refer to something different; to the guaranteed freedoms or immunities (from royal or baronial interference) of a corporate entity which cuts across states, like the Church, or which exists within the state, like a city or guild. [11]

Lewis then refers to two things—both he stated are unparalleled in ancient language and startling things. If a medieval serf became a member of any corporation or city that is free, that serf became free and shared in freedom. And freedom can mean citizenship, as when Saint Paul at a great price obtained his Roman citizenship.

Finally, Lewis analyzed the word *liberal* as a cultural term finding a Greek, Latin and English connection that is not relevant for our purposes, but illustrates how liberal education evolved from Aristotle to various English authors. This topic alone justifies several books on liberal education that cannot be relevantly pursued here.

The most creative aspect of C. S. Lewis is his insistence that we note how different is a medieval reference to freedom compared with the classical Greek or Roman reference to freedom of a city-state or the empire, or of freedom from subjection to a foreign power. There is such an extraordinary degree of historical meaning packed into a few sentences of Lewis that the significance would escape most persons unfamiliar with the history of medieval Europe. But, once again, our labors of understanding are given an astronomical boost by the work of Harold Berman in his *Law and Revolution* (1983). He questioned just how different is the idea of freedom in Europe as it evolved from Roman meanings to meanings in the Middle Ages, the Reformation and beyond in time.

Berman wove important threads of history together as he explained the "Formation of the Western Legal Tradition." The narrowness of American concepts of law blocks a vision of a social theory of law he propounded. And part of this historical record reveals a connection among city charters of liberties, the Magna Carta, slavery, serfdom and peasantry. Manorial law for peasant relations and peasant revolts are a part of this complex mosaic.

For the purposes of defining freedom, there is no need to offer a summary of Berman's 600-page book, nor would that do him justice or offer to the reader any sense of the depth of his work. My aim is to offer only an immense clue found in the seminal work of Berman that will make C. S. Lewis's comments on freedom more meaningful.

The church-state struggle of the Middle Ages is important for our discussion. Canon law was developed by the Church—the Catholic Church. Mercantile law, royal law, manorial and urban law were developed by others. Businesses developed mercantile law, for example. Slavery was commonly practiced in Europe, and there developed a form of peasantry who were neither free nor slaves, which included free peasants, slaves and serfs. These people worked the land for the lord of the manor, and helped evolve a complex set of superior- subordinate relationships. To quote Berman, "European serfs in the eleventh and twelfth centuries were for the first time in a strong enough position to take the risk of illegal escape from their lords to other lords who offered better working conditions." [12] By late 13th and 14th centuries, there were widespread peasant rebellions and large scale manumissions of serfs in France, Germany and England. As peasants deserted the manor, its various systems broke down and the charters of liberties of emerging cities protected former serfs, peasants and slaves who escaped to cities. Most European cities were founded by an act or charter that established basic "liberties" of citizens, usually including rights of self-government. Legal and religious factors were closely linked in this process. People as well as churches could now span national boundaries. Thus, thoroughly documented by Berman, urbanization was a major factor in defining liberty in Europe in city after city. In a similar way, the contemporary human rights movement is evidence of a global development of a common meaning for worldwide citizenship. This modern event parallels the serf of the Middle Ages who got his freedom by escaping to a city, the way people move from nation to nation today seeking freedom.

Hidden within a delightful account by C. S. Lewis of the origin and development of the words *free, liberal* and *frank* are a couple of thousand years of European development that has some significant bearing on our use of the same ideas. Both Berman's historical account and our own sense of history tell us that the meaning of liberty and freedom has seen a world that none of us today will ever experience in either geography or time. From a perspective called sociological history, Orlando Patterson conveys some of the same medieval reality in Chapters 20-22 of his 1991 book *Freedom.* The seeds for the new paradigm of freedom that are to be developed next are found in this history just mentioned.

TRANSFORMATION OF FREEDOM

How much time is left to write what we think is the truth? The lease on life is indefinite in time, but we are sure of one thing—the lease on life is not infinite or timeless. The pressure of a short life when study takes so long (*vita brevis—studium longum*) means that truth may be eclipsed by the shadow of time on one's ability to think. Far too many reflections on human freedom are a product of a short attention span, a shifting emphasis, or a breezy reflection on matters that require many years of patient study and mature reflection. Decade-long projects are not common, but neither are they rare; one frequently reads of authors who spend decades thinking thoughts through. A splendid example is Margaret Yourcenar in *Memoirs of Hadrian* which began in 1924 as an idea and finally culminated in publication in 1951 with other editions, the one in English emerging in 1963. Nearly four decades of emergence from the mind's womb—a long birth for ideas. This is honorable work at its best.

Similarly, this book about human freedom has a long gestation period going back to the early 1960s when I first read Herbert Muller's *Freedom in the Ancient World.*[13] He followed with several more volumes on freedom. His reference was to Pericles of Athens (494-429 B.C.) in the famous *Funeral Oration* (431 B.C.) for soldiers who protected Athens. That oration was one of the earliest expressions in Western Civilization in which one could identify a living ideal of freedom or *eleutheria*, as the Greeks called it. The ideal intrigued me. The ancient Greeks have attracted the attention of mankind for 2,500 years, and the attraction continues to this day. Many of our words are still closely tied to Greco/Latin origins. Though we have lost the ancient Greek and Latin languages in our common knowledge, there is still much to learn from ancient Greeks, especially on the subject of human liberty. It is no secret that civic education in America needs a revitalization of its intellectual roots, especially its understanding of ancient roots of freedom. The principal concern here is to explore this risky urge to independence in an ancient people.

As Max Pohlenz, a classical scholar, said so eloquently of the ancient Greeks:

It was the tragedy of the Greek people that the very characteristic to which they owed their greatness [freedom] when carried to excess became their undoing. Just as in the relations of the city-states with each other, the aversion to all restraint led to a separation which prevented the unification of the nation, similarly within the state the urge to freedom, once aroused, led to an individualism demanding the right of the individual "to live as he liked." In consequence liberty degenerated into license, resisting any obligation, regarding authority as compulsion, and thus undermining public order. The individual no longer felt himself a member of the whole, but a partner with equal rights, so that the state became an organization of men looked upon as a welfare institution without feeling towards it any of the old sense of duty. The consequence was the loss of national independence.[14]

Pohlenz's reflection is on the ancient Greek ideal of freedom for some men only—and how it led the Athenians to a "loss of national independence." Jacques Barzun recently could see a similar pattern in the world's nations today as either breaking up or breaking down—a virulent rage for absolute freedom. He was not certain what to call the blazing phenomena of separatism that is so prevalent among nations around the world.[15] Barzun wrote in 1989: "In short, the one political and social ideal, the one motive power of the time is Separatism, no matter what other rags of older philosophy it masquerades under. If this is not yet Breakdown, it is undeniably Breakup."[16]

Across the globe are aspirations for self-determination, for self-government, for a struggle for freedom and the desire is for autonomy, which the Greeks called *autonomia*. As Cynthia Farrar said, Pericles, in the famous *Funeral Oration*, stigmatized men who took no part in politics by calling them *useless*. Cynthia Farrar states:

Autonomy depends upon the active participation and daring willingness to take risks characteristic of men who prize self-determination. The democratic freedoms and responsibilities well expressed in the term "self-rule" or giving laws to oneself (*auto-nomos*) are deemed essential to the freedom of the city and all its citizens. Self-determination is the only form of rule compatible with freedom.[17]

The Greek passion for freedom from foreign domination by Turkey expressed itself in more modern times through Lord Byron who said, "Yet Freedom! yet thy banner, torn but flying, Streams like the thunder storm against the wind." Victor Ehrenberg in *Man, State and Diety* (1974) was also clear on this point:

In the language of diplomacy since 1918 it became the small nation's right of self-determination. It was this that broke up the Hapsburg empire, it is this that lives again in the explosive aspirations of the so-called developing countries. Here are great opportunities and great dangers, dangers for the individual state and for the society of states as a whole. May be, freedom among the nations is just a dream, and in the last resort perhaps not even a good one. But history is not concerned with that. History shows time and again that a people would rather have self-government, with all its difficulties and uncertainties, than live under foreign rule no matter how well meaning.[18]

There is vitality to a way of life when you "know thyself," in the best Socratic tradition, and when you "give laws to yourself"—you are autonomos. *Nomos* is the ideal the Greeks called law. And Immanuel Kant in the late 1700s in one of his famous categorical imperatives reminds us that we are free in inner life—our subjective life—if we give laws to ourselves that we would obey ourselves. And greater yet, we would obey laws we make for others, that is, as legislators and judges and governors we are bound by the same laws we make. There is not one law for the governor and another for the governed; one for the rich and another for the poor; not one law for the high and mighty and another for the lowly.

Where the Greeks stimulated the intelligent world most successfully is into an understanding of the significance of community against alien domination—foreign domination and loss of freedom. Before, during and after every war, the fear of loss of this freedom is very powerful in societies, ancient and modern. The Greek city-state was vulnerable to attack if alone, so in ancient Greece, leagues of city-states were formed—an attack on one was an attack on the others. Does this remind you of NATO and the Warsaw Pact alliances during the Cold War? Does it remind you of all the other global alliances and associations? Today we still confront the perpetual problem of small states being gobbled up by bigger states. The freedom to survive as a nation is significant. The "breakdown" that Barzun saw in 1989 immediately became a reality. Ask Kuwait in 1993. Iraq attacked Kuwait and mercilessly decimated it in August 1990, laid waste to oil fields, raped and plundered. Iraq was then violently attacked in the 1991 Persian Gulf War by a twenty-eight-nation group through United Nations auspices. By February 27, 1991, a unilateral cease fire was declared. Five thousand years ago in the same land, the same acts of violence between tribes and kingdoms happened. The biblical "wars and rumors of wars" still dominated the disquietude of the 20th century—wars made in the name of freedom, some in the name of greed, jealousy and hunger for power or domination and oil wealth. Potential trouble is exacerbated today by having so many vulnerable little nations. These are the risks Ehrenberg suggested.

What was just explored is national liberty of the state from other states. This aspect of freedom is ideal and real; it is basic; it stirs our deepest emotion of loyalty to the community; and it challenges us to think of the serious and dangerous conditions in statelessness of a human being. What will an enemy do to you if it conquers you? People without citizenship in some nation are stateless—quite free, but terribly exposed to whatever trouble 178 or more nations can dream up for aliens, strangers and noncitizens. It is so important in the United States to have United States citizenship that the United States Constitution has been interpreted by the Supreme Court to deny the federal government the right to take away citizenship.[19] It is forbidden, cruel and unusual punishment under the Eighth Amendment to denaturalize citizens of the United States. Quite simply—it cannot be done as a form of punishment even though the greater paradox of death sentences are allowed. The Eighth Amendment and its interpretation forbids the United States government from creating stateless people of its citizens. This is utterly basic to life—a lifetime membership by birth or naturalization in a nation called the United States of America is a minimum liberty. This is freedom to be part of a state in a world of other nation states to which external freedom is linked.

VICTOR EHRENBERG—DIVIDING AN IDEAL

The idea of freedom is more than the idea of such protective national liberty, for a state to protect itself and its integrity with regard to other states or foreign nationals or refugees. Perhaps a clear, acceptable, easily understood and practical way to think of liberty is to break liberty or freedom into three parts.
1. Liberty of the state: was defined as national freedom above, national and popular sovereignty in its legal, democratic and historical sense in a global setting.

2.   Liberty *within* a state: to take part in its political life—to vote, to hold office, to be a juror, to govern in some way, to not be a slave or not to be tortured.

3.   Liberty *from* a state: to express one's ideas—an inner liberty; to paint, to speak freely, to write freely, to associate with whomever we wish, to travel where we desire, to conduct family life as we see fit, to have or not have children, to express religious ideas, to refrain from religion completely, and so on.

Victor Ehrenberg is one major source of these ideas of yet another "tripartite" definition of liberty, one which greatly appeals to me.

The Greeks have taught us what liberty could be, and that it is not a gift of nature but something to be fought for. It was an ideal, and as such indivisible. In modern times, however, a distinction has been made between several concepts of liberty, and this is useful, even though no full agreement has been reached. We can speak of three different yet associated types of liberty. First, there is liberty of the state (national freedom), the freedom of a community from alien domination or despotism. Secondly, there is the political liberty of the citizen within the state. And thirdly, there is personal liberty, the independence of the individual. The latter includes, for example, the artist's freedom of expression which is perhaps the purest form of this kind of liberty.[20]

The unity of the idea of freedom in a Platonic sense has been so important (as an ideal) that I resisted for a long time the three-way division of Ehrenberg, Pohlenz and even Orlando Patterson in his *Freedom* (1991). Mortimer Adler's five-way division of freedom confuses me even though it may accurately reflect history. Furthermore, it is not appealing because it seems to be an opaque definition, and it seems to result in an ending of urgency of understanding of the idea of freedom. Isaiah Berlin offers too little definition in his obtuse tome. These different approaches are valuable, but none expresses what seems to me to be true, easily understood and practical. All of them are deficient from an American historical, legal, and political perspective. However, all are strong from a general historical, philosophical, and sociological viewpoint. Then, on balance Ehrenberg offers a united framework that suggests most clearly how the ideal of freedom has three aspects, but that each aspect dovetails into the other aspects or parts of freedom. Think of the three parts as three strings on a violin, banjo or mandolin. Think of harmony if you know how to play the instrument. The state is the structure or violin frame—good, bad or indifferent and it is part of the picture by providing a structure threatening, helpful and indifferent to freedom.

The definition of liberty or freedom requires an examination of the "architecture" of freedom, its structure which then needs to be fleshed out.

In the final part of this chapter we will examine the transformation of structure into its contingent relationship with other values. We will concentrate on what I call processes of conflict or cooperation between freedom with other sets of important values—authority, property, equality, justice and privacy.

ARCHITECTURE OF FREEDOM—TRANSFORMED PARADIGM

The architecture of freedom is an avenue of analysis; it tells in clearer terms what the design of freedom has grown to be for one of the most complex ideas that man uses. Not unlike the many systems that make up a skyscraper, the systems of freedom contribute to an integrated structure. As a skyscraper needs a solid foundation so does the architecture of freedom need a solid foundation. A skyscraper needs elevators and stairs to link it together for movement. So does the architecture of freedom need connectors among its parts so that we know when we are discussing an aspect of freedom; we all agree that when we are on the fourteenth floor we are not in the basement. The architectural design of a skyscraper is not the real thing; the design of the idea of freedom is not the reality that people experience. The design of freedom is on paper and in records, and it results in human actions; but it is not a physical structure—the result of an architectural design of a skyscraper. Designing and building skyscrapers results in a tangible building—a modern masterpiece of human thought, human action and real-world materials. A building you can touch and experience is the result. A consequence of the idea of freedom can never be touched unless it is translated in some way into a tangible object. The Statue of Liberty in New York Harbor is a tangible outcome of the idea of freedom felt in America and Europe—in France where it was built, and in the United States where it was located on an island and on a base resulting from joint resources on the North American continent. But much more frequently, freedom has no tangible outcome like a Statue of Liberty.

Karl Popper offers an explanation for the reality of freedom that is more persuasive than any other of which I am aware. Essentially, Popper argues for a concept of reality composed of three worlds.[21] World I is physical nature—the air, the globe earth, all that can be sensed, seen, heard, touched, tasted and smelled. It includes the people on earth in their physical being. World II is the special world open only to mankind—the psychological world of ideas, feelings and nonphysical phenomena (a metaphysical phenomena), and here is where freedom exists in a real form. World III is created by mankind and found in paintings of animals on the walls of Lascaux in southern France some 20,000 years ago; Symphony no. 9 by Beethoven; the idea of love in Christian charity; the idea of gravity from Newton; the idea of a solar system from Copernicus and Galileo; the idea of germs from Leeuwenhoek; the idea of writing; the wheel; the uses of fire, etc. These ideas are intergenerationally independent of their creators—such as algebraic, geometric and chemical formulas, writing, books, designs, plays, sculpture, computer programs, files and tapes in which man deposits his intellectual outcomes, an intelligible form for permanent accretion to the human knowledge bank. A right triangle is a right triangle everywhere on earth. Libraries, museums, art galleries, and other places store objects and understandings of World III. Much that mankind has experienced with regard to freedom can be found in World III. The research for this book rests significantly on more than a decade of systematic searching for what others have thought and said and written about freedom in World III. And it is important to say the search was for evidence of all kinds—not just evidence to support a particular vision of freedom that I concocted as a basic thesis for the research underlying this book. A World III architectural sketch of freedom is needed to understand the basic design:

Architecture of Freedom

National Freedom
- Associated with:
  —Multinational corporations
  —Ideas of sovereignty, alien, citizen
  —International groupings
  —United Nations, other international trade order and agreements
  —War and peace
  —Nationalism and treason
  —Feeling of loyalty to group.

Freedom Within a State
- Associated with:
  —Meanings of citizenship
  —Voting
  —Democracy
  —Representative bodies
  —Federalism, separation of powers and decentralized powers
  —Rights not to be tortured or put to death.

Freedom From a State
- Associated with:
  —Natural law and Antigone
  —Private property
  —Privacy and personal autonomy
  —Artistic freedom
  —Freedom of association
  —Free enterprise
  —Freedom of press
  —Freedom of speech
  —Freedom of religion
  —Academic freedom.

The structure of freedom requires more explanation than the outline above provides.

NATIONAL FREEDOM—FREEDOM FROM ALIEN DOMINATION AND DESPOTISM

How can we distinguish these three aspects of freedom from one another? First, national freedom is the clearest idea; it is the foundation for nationalism as a global phenomena; there is an international focus to this type of freedom. There are poignant statements about national freedom 2,500 years old in Pericles' *Funeral Oration*. War-time appeals are especially notable in this arena; Lord Byron during the long Greek struggle for liberation; Churchill during World War II; and many others. The United Nations focuses upon national sovereignty in its deliberations even though it also gave birth to the Declaration of Human Rights in 1948, a matter more relevant to the other two parts of freedom, and the 1993 Vienna Declaration on Human Rights.

National freedom is significant to a much greater degree when a nation is about to be born or is in its early life. Thereafter, when nationhood is threatened by some force—internal, via subversion or external, by military threat—then does the concern for national sovereignty arise. This is recognized as "political freedom," but such a term is useless to identify anything—it is just too vague. American's lack of willingness to vote is further evidence that when there is no external threat to a group of people who call itself a nation, then Orlando Patterson's similar "civic freedom" loses its attraction and allure for citizens. Nations that are complacent—fat, happy and unchallenged—those complacently self-satisfied are not places where the interest in national freedom is of paramount concern. Such national freedom has been achieved already. There is nothing further to conquer to achieve such freedom. There is no sense of struggle as if sitting on a pin. Here national freedom survives, but it may be a boring subject; it could put people to sleep! Even though national sovereignty is now nightmarishly expensive in terms of weapons of war, it is the sovereignty that is widely threatened today—as in:

Quebec v. Canada (tension)
Czech Federal Republic v. Slovakia (now broken apart)
Muslim v. Croat v. Serb (in former Yugoslavia)
Long list of new "nations" separated off in last forty years since the United Nations began—especially in Africa as colonial power ended.

Certainly freedom—"national freedom"—is a kind or type of freedom that is a separate idea from freedom within a nation or state, or freedom from a state in the third sense of the word freedom—individual autonomy.

FREEDOM WITHIN A NATION

The second aspect of freedom is within a nation or state. The focus is national in scope and the international attention is minimal. Freedom within a state is evident in the social contract between citizens and a state experienced in written law in most advanced societies. The constitutional statement and amendments express the bargain struck between citizens in their social contract to which they all belong in a community. The idea of freedom within a nation rests upon constitutional order and positive law order found in statutes or legislation expressive of popular majority views found in such laws. The idea of national sovereignty is accepted, but it is further subdivided so that both forms of freedom—further freedom—could survive in a society. The freedom of political subdivisions is expressed either by federalism or other forms of unity of the state. Separation of powers expresses the diffusion of power inside branches of political units. The concepts of federalism and separation of powers are major power channeling ideas that are relevant to freedom within a nation. More analysis in Chapter 6 will clarify these assertions. And common law often offers a route to a more just civil order where freedom is taken into account.

Most significant are the limits on this second aspect of freedom within a state. The condition of being free is deeply affected by the presence or absence of a social contract premised upon a Bill of Rights. The end of state power is found here when an individual right begins. The flavor of a democracy is found in this branch of freedom. The political right to hold office, to vote on officials and issues—the core of representative government is significant to a definition of this second type of freedom within a state. Being a juror is a significant part of this aspect. Freedom in France compared with freedom in South Africa in the sense of freedom within the state is significantly different—as different for black Americans as freedom in Mississippi in 1930 compared with freedom in New York in 1930.

FREEDOM FROM THE NATION OR STATE

The third branch of the definition of freedom is freedom *from* a state. The *Casey* decision on abortion illustrates this in Chapter 4. The focus in this branch is individual in nature. *Antigone* in Sophocles' play in 445 B.C. represents one of the oldest expressions of the freedom from the state represented by monarch King Creon who commands that Antigone's brother lie unburied on a battlefield due to treachery Creon believed to be true of the dead warrior. Antigone, as a sister, believed a higher law commanded her to bury her brother rather than see his remains eaten by birds and dogs. The innate respect for the dead human body is a near universal—and freedom to bury the dead is what the living believe is their duty regardless of what a tyrant or majority of a legislative body may say. The real question is how many other subjects are "beyond legislation," "beyond state control," "beyond the competence of a state." John Stuart Mill and John Locke would argue that there is much beyond state control.

The ideas associated with freedom from a state call into play a more abstract vision of man and state. The source of law is natural law found in a person's reasoning power or natural reasoning power—a Ciceronian, Roman 100 A.D. vision of state incompetence and private domains.

The civil law and common-law character, the national law character and the focus on individuality and human autonomy from any form of state control in certain "spheres of liberty," to use Kammen's logic, are the primary focus of this kind of freedom. Here all seems to be beyond the social contract, where there is nothing paramount to the individual's solitary choice to define freedom. Freedom to commit suicide is of such a character, especially if in terminal illness. And there is significant dispute in America about this—especially physician-assisted termination of one's life. Freedom to decide to abort a fetus within certain time parameters is in this same controversial zone. Does a woman have such a "natural right" to control her own body under such limited circumstances, free of state control and majority rule?   A great number of Americans—male and female—believe in this "natural right" of choice. Although some call the right a "constitutional right" they also mean a natural right in the historical sense of the words "natural right."

In America, there is a double problem with individual sovereignty to decide for one's self a wide range of issues with absolutely *no* state sovereign interference. Here a person is a sovereign in the sense Mill argued. And it is here that confusion reigns supreme in the American citizens of the nation, in visitors who see America and, especially, in young people in America who are trying to understand just exactly of what their freedom consists. There is *no* social contract to examine the nature of such freedom because freedom from the state is beyond the contract. Such individual sovereignty is idiosyncratic, personal, unrelated to other people, quite often in the artistic arena, and highly troublesome to social conformists or "control freaks" who are terribly worried about such "uncontrolled" freedom who see not freedom, but anarchy—private anarchy—a soulless devotion to individualism of self-destruction. About this much more will be said in Chapter 6.

Freedom *from* a state or nation means that police can do nothing, legislatures cannot make law, judges have no power to decide any issues, no prisons or jails can be brought to bear to enforce any custom, norm, rule of interest to outsiders. This branch of freedom is so frightening to some people they refuse to acknowledge its existence. There is a fear of this freedom from the state that is parallel to a fear of terrorist activities, and there may even be a parallel belief system—that people who claim such inner freedom from the state are terrorists in fact and must be suppressed for the good of the known social order under laws and constitutions. Many in America reacted to fear of communistic subversion with an inquisitorial thought control strategy.

The fear of the lawless mob is not an irrational fear. The law-abiding know what riots mean—a breakdown that could lead to anarchy without superior force. Somalia in 1992 with its fifteen or more tribal factions is a prime example. Lebanon in the 1980s is another; ex-Yugoslavia in 1993 is a third. These examples of great or total collapse of authority or order requires one to say in each case that national freedom is gone, freedom inside or within a state is gone because the state has disappeared. And certainly freedom from a state, complete hyper-freedom is all that is left—a highly dangerous condition for human life not unlike being alone in high wilderness, at sea, or on a small island. Individual sovereignty is guaranteed, but it is not worth having in any measure for other reasons—the extraordinary risks of survival alone in the weather without food or water, often in the midst of some form of war. The fear of the looter is obvious after social fabric of law and order is dissolved by mass destruction of hurricanes Iniki, Andrew, Hugo and others, and by wars in Somalia and Lebanon and other national disasters.

The freedom from a state is sensible when a state exists in a strong form and with full power so that national freedom and freedom within a state coexist. It is almost as if it is impossible to dwell on freedom from a state, say in privacy issues, unless the state is externally powerful. Without a state, there is no value in privacy, for all is private and then the most powerful private interest wins such contests where no social contract exists. A state with some considerable power must be the premise to freedom from a state.

There is a zone of privacy now being recognized—as in Amish religious decisions to keep their children out of public schools after a certain age, though other children must attend a public school. In religious affairs, there is an end to state control. Decisions of great significance to a person—what they will or will not eat or drink—is an example. What they will read, what church to attend or whether to abstain from religion, whether to marry, these and many more areas of freedom exist, thrive and are becoming clearer over time as the state attempts to become more and more controlling via positive law. The *Casey* decision discussed in Chapter 4 is, also an example of privacy. Natural rights of people are a barrier to state action or federal action. And these natural rights are not definable by the state which can recognize them or not as they appear. They are constitutional Ninth Amendment rights reserved to the people. The unknown dimension of the freedom from a state is an exciting quality—precisely the same quality of excitement that one experiences in delightfulness of genius. Genius has no boundaries—human discovery would never be a reality if a state defined the intellectual limits of freedom from a state. The Catholic Church tried such intellectual control; it finally acknowledged in 1992 its error in suppressing Galileo.

Ultimately we are reduced to the question in this third area of freedom, who shall define such freedom from the state? Shall the state or a religious group define the scope or limits of freedom from the state? Or, shall each individual decide for him- or herself what is the limit or scope of such freedom? How to decide the question is the central problem of freedom defined as freedom from a state. Freedom within a state presumes a powerful role for the state in defining liberty. National freedom likewise presumes a powerful existence and role for the nation or state in the international arena. This is *not* the case in freedom from a state where the role of the state is in question—whether the state belongs or not is the true question for the individual. Women making the abortion decision understand this issue intimately. And it is here that Kammen's analysis could be applied with some logically relevant application. Under conditions where every person is a law giver in Kant's sense of personal autonomy, what kinds of individual decisions are appropriate:

1.   Decisions that will not seriously disrupt the authority and order of the state?
2.   Decisions that will not destroy the notion of private property?
3.   Decisions that will not increase the likelihood of riots and serious civil disorder?
4.   Decisions that will seem to be just to many people—not merely a few?
5.   Decisions that will not greatly upset the equality in the society?
6.   Decisions that will fit into privacy of citizens—enlarging their private autonomous decision-making spheres?

These three aspects of freedom—national freedom, freedom within a state, and freedom from a state—are each quite different from one another. Conflicts over one type of freedom may not affect other types of freedom. For example, freedom to choose or avoid a particular religion may be inner liberty. A decision to travel abroad is the same, but there may be an effect among types of freedom where religious belief (say against abortion) may color another citizen's decision to have an abortion who herself has no connection with an organized religious group. Here, in the latter example, one view (religious) may oppose another view of abortion (personal—not religiously related). In this example, the state has little role to play; it is an area where keeping the peace is the only role, not enforcing one religious view or nonreligious as opposed to another. Freedom from the state for one person depends upon the state's action to enforce individual autonomy over an organized religious viewpoint that opposes such action. Abortion conflict is of this character, and it is a type of inner liberty—clearly distinguished from national freedom and freedom within a state. Here is a clarity that I hope the new transformed idea of freedom can lead to some resolution of some abortion conflict. The limits of state power are the central feature of freedom from a state. How much inner liberty we have is another way to see the opposite side of freedom from a state.

It is not enough to clarify the ideal of freedom into three distinctive parts as was just done in this chapter. The question remains that was stated at the beginning of the book, *Is liberty a contingent value and not preeminent?* Is liberty conditioned frequently on, or in conflict with, other human values such as equality and justice? One of America's most significant voices thought liberty was contingent not absolute or preeminent—Walter Lippmann. He asserted this truth in 1920. Let us examine this aspect next.

TRANSFORMED FREEDOM AND OTHER VALUES: CONTINGENT FREEDOM

Michael Kammen summed up his *Spheres of Liberty* by stating in another—the second most important of observations in this book:

We also needed to rediscover in the twentieth century what John Winthrop understood so well in the seventeenth, James Madison in the eighteenth and Abraham Lincoln in the nineteenth: *that liberty cannot be defined or appreciated as a singular quality.* Walter Lippmann epitomized the point in 1920: "I can recall no doctrine of liberty," he wrote, "which, under the acid test, does not become contingent upon some other ideal." That has, indeed, been the quintessential character of liberty's ever-changing role in American culture (Emphasis added).[22]

The soundness of Lippmann's and Kammen's conclusion is, or should be, obvious from the preceding analysis. To make the point as clearly as possible: freedom is structured into three parts—national freedom, freedom within a state, and freedom from the state. But these basic aspects of freedom must be seen also in the more complex light that history casts upon them. The eloquence of liberty spokesmen is greatest when national freedom is threatened: Pericles' *Funeral Oration* in 430-31 B.C.; Churchill's call to arms in World War II to the British people; Franklin D. Roosevelt's contempt for the "dastardly" armed strike on Pearl Harbor by Japanese pilots and empire on December 7, 1941—"a date that will live in infamy."

The eloquence of liberty spokesmen seems less powerful in the second field of freedom within a state, but it has many forms: The Civil Rights Act of 1964; the Amendment to the United States Constitution allowing women to vote; the Amendment to the United States Constitution forbidding slavery in 1865; the Supreme Court decision to require police to give Miranda warnings to people suspected of crime. The decision in *Roe v. Wade* is freedom from the state to recognize the personal autonomy and privacy of women to make the decision to abort without state interference. Amending the United States Constitution to allow progressive taxation of incomes by the federal government is a clear rich-poor classical decision where the majority won a constitutional amendment and a series of statutes, the rich lost permanently in the United States because a Constitutional limit was put on their power to earn and ultimately to keep their wealth. Billionaires will pay very high taxes; their freedom to act is constrained, but society protects their wealth in exchange for the loss of some economic liberty. Liberty challenges property rights quite effectively, and the reverse is true.

These channeling values—as Walter Lippmann said, are the contingent ideals that interact with liberty: namely authority, order, property, justice, equality and privacy which have an enormous bearing on the quality, extent and direction of freedom in any society at a particular moment in time. The linking of a structure of freedom with processes that channel freedom's growth, development or demise is often, *I repeat often* ignored in a static, abstract and excessively impersonal "objective" account of freedom. It is also lost in civil libertarian logic of liberty, although there are frequently recognitions that two liberties may clash; "fair trial and free press" is an example among others. Some analyses of freedom cause paralysis by excessive analyses. Deadening of imagination is hardly desirable.

Dynamic tension was experienced by the classical Greeks in the bow and arrow and the lyre. The way to think about freedom in its three formal structures is to see it in dynamic tension with other values over time. World war, civil unrest, civil internal war, famine, natural disaster, all of these forces of nature and forces of mankind are durable features of the landscape in which human beings exist. The new paradigm of freedom takes them into account. The value of freedom to a human being is not merely one remote ideal in a Platonic sense of the word ideal. The value of freedom is more than a July Fourth celebration of national freedom and a look at the Statue of Liberty and fireworks.

It is a fundamental error to suppose that freedom (in its three meanings) can be a human value that knows no limit, yet there are some who argue this way. The most common argument centers around personal autonomy of the super rich rock star and Hollywood star and society's constraints. Their using drugs and alcohol to excess is not unknown. Their using women who are "groupies" is not unheard of. Their using the society for any personal whims is within their power so they think—some of them. This observation is not intended to denigrate all Hollywood and rock stars, but given their wide notoriety, level of education, maturity, civility and cultivated grasp of civilization, coupled sometimes with their simplistic notion of freedom from any control—there then arises a typical twenty-year personal struggle obvious to anyone, until Mother Nature ages the body and soul of a rock star or Hollywood star. Even the aging Hollywood stars, if they survive, understand freedom better, not as a license, but as an ordered liberty.

Another way to see or to understand the dynamic tension between freedom and its three principal structures and freedom in its clash with values of equal importance, at a particular time in the life of a society, is to think of divergencies. Some call these contradictions "antinomies"—an admission that opposite viewpoints each have some validity and truth. A divergency, as I prefer to call them, at a society-wide level is wanting maximum free speech, but not so free as to trigger riots and cause human destruction. Another example is wanting freedom of religion but not so free that parents may end medical care available to children that need it to live. A further example, wanting safe streets but not so safe that cops can beat citizens the way they beat up Rodney King in Los Angeles. Wanting a good thing, and wanting another good thing but having one to excess that could exclude the other, is the classical problem of absolute equality vs. absolute liberty. Poised on each side of this divergency are advocates who say any movement on the other side threatens their equality or liberty depending upon which side they are on. For example, the "have-nots" dominate the voting in societies filled with a much smaller number of very wealthy other citizens. The power of the majority in a democracy to level the rich through taxation (in another context the power to tax is "the power to destroy" was heard at one time in the United States of America from the rich) is a very obvious divergency. A capitalistic, free enterprise society prizes maximum freedom from taxes for the rich; the "have-nots" idealize economic equality and push for progressive taxation to equalize life in a society. Liberty is limited by equality in such a contest; this fight is *the undercurrent* of much political tension in any society. That such a divergency is universal was recognized thousands of years ago when Hammurabi said rich and poor must both be accommodated under law in a civilization. Is there a better perspective? Let us next add some further analogies and analysis.

PROCESSES OF FREEDOM

Here in this part of the chapter, we move from structure to process within the idea of freedom, whether national freedom, freedom within a state or freedom from state action. To use architectural analogies, I think of processes in a dynamic sense—the movement of water, the movement of electricity, the movement of hot and cold air, the movement of messages via telephone lines, computers, and so forth. The analogy is a bit strained, but the clashes of freedom with other human values of equivalent important stature mean that the energy of freedom gets channeled like water, electricity and air in a skyscraper. What are these competing, contingent, important values? Some use the word "responsibility" to mean something that must be joined to freedom. "Responsibility" can further be defined in the following manner of competing values to freedom.

Freedom and Authority

For example, when conditions in a state become chaotic, disorganized and the state is headed toward dissolution—Somalia in 1992 is an example—its freedom has run into a need for authority to re-establish a state; the value of authority creates channels and confines national freedom and freedom within a state. Freedom from a state or the remnants of a state in armed gangs is a worthless freedom. It is difficult to think of civil authority as a system to confine freedom, but what else is it? When civil war was about to arise in the United States, the authority of federal government dropped in the south but rose in the north. When authority and the order it imposes were needed during the Civil War, then President Lincoln suspended the writ of habeas corpus—making it impossible to contest in court the seizure and imprisonment of citizens. And yet the north sought freedom for blacks by ending slavery. Freedom is confined by a greater need to have "law and order," that is, to have authority and order. The best historical evidence of this is found in Michael Kammen's *Spheres of Liberty*.

His examples illustrate the important point that freedom and liberty are seriously confined in periods when other needs are felt to be more paramount or important in a society. Freedom is not an unchallenged supreme value in the Western Civilization under all circumstances, particularly war time. Freedom is contingent sometimes.

Freedom and Property

When a capitalistic economy rises, based on private property, then autonomous free-enterprise corporate giants arise and protection of their private property is a critical concern. Most of the valuable property (i.e., manufacturing plants, planes) in the United States is owned by the Fortune 500 corporations. Here Kammen illustrates how a fear for freedom of property generated many restrictions on the state. A freedom from the state would become the battle cry of wealthy liberals and conservatives. The idea of private property stops governmental taking of private property without just compensation required by the Fifth Amendment of the United States Constitution. This is currently a "hot button" topic among some conservatives, but it has also, always been a concern of thoughtful conservative economists like Friedrich A. Hayek in *The Constitution of Liberty* (1960).

Freedom to take other people's property is frightening in its implications at any level. State seizure of private property was action taken by communists in Cuba when they took over. Nationalizing of industry during war is common. After hurricane Andrew demolished south Florida, the looters began and so did armed forces of the state—"shooting to kill looters." Television vividly captures looters in Los Angeles and Miami. Armed military force was inserted to stop the chaos of a freedom to steal. Freedom to steal was stopped dead in its tracks by the idea of private property backed by the armed might of the state, by men with guns in their hands. But Harry S. Truman, president of the United States, sought to "nationalize" the steel mills, and he was stopped by constitutional decision of the Supreme Court—unless he paid for the steel mills.[23] He never found the authority from Congress or the cash. Freedom is not a paramount, unchallenged value in Western Civilization when it comes to private property that must be paid for when the government wants it. The boundary for freedom is private property in a capitalist order.

Freedom and Equality

There is little doubt that a classless, absolutely equal society of all men, women and children would constrain freedom of many adult males—men who have most of the power in most societies, if not all. Women, children and minorities would gain power across the globe by having greater equality. A theoretical, absolute equality is a value that creates processes to limit freedom. The formula is rather simple. The more that equality is desired as a value, the less that liberty and differences based on individual liberty will be available to those who must be leveled or changed to achieve greater equality. James MacGregor Burns identified this struggle as central to America's history. Usually the greatest good—equality—serves the greatest number of people and the fewer people experience less freedom. Equality is a channeler of freedom—the Equal Employment Opportunity Act in the United States of America is an excellent example. But so is the equal right to vote, the equal right to sit on a jury—all freedoms within a state are subjected to this channeling power of equality. Equality has been the great tool of everyone in America who fought chattel slavery of the Negro as an institution. The rice and tobacco plantation owners in the pre-Civil War southern states were changed or leveled and so were many of their mansions leveled during the Civil War. The power of equality channels some peoples' freedom to make way for freedom for other people in a state. And the state itself is premised on equality, and restrictions of freedom are a valid part of state aims.

Kammen offers a series of delightful examples in his *Spheres of Liberty* of the power of equality when its conflicts with liberty. The American Civil War is the preeminent example where the definition of liberty went through a paradigm shift forced by equality of new black citizens.

Freedom and Justice

Capturing, trying, convicting and imprisoning of fellow citizens is otherwise thought to be the work of a "criminal justice system" in America and elsewhere. Human freedom is most clearly channeled when a society strives to create justice between fellow citizens who are victims of murder, rape, robbery, burglary, theft, fraud—the list is long of wrongs done by one citizen against another that a society labels "a crime." True, also, is justice in civil wrongs—broken contracts, physical injury to others by negligence, disputes over property ownership—all of the civil disputes need attention and channeling to achieve justice. Justice confines freedom. Kammen gives some examples of freedom and justice in contention. One such example in recent times is forcing the state for the sake of justice to hire lawyers to defend poor people accused of crimes under the Sixth Amendment to the Constitution of the United States.

Freedom and Privacy

Where the state ends, where state power no longer operates, one could presume that a zone of privacy exists in which a human being makes personal, autonomous decisions unrelated to what a state may articulate as its majority beliefs in laws.[24] The end to majority and community rule is tested every day under bills of rights that explicitly stop the government, the majority, from doing anything it pleases with citizens. The idea that there are limits to government is not within the ideas available to citizens in a tyranny—say Iraq in 1992 or many other less-tyrannical nations where civil rights and human rights under the United Nations Declaration of Rights in 1948 are ignored. These nations include religion-dominated governments in Iran in 1992 (extraterritorial threats to author Rushdie) to Kuwait in 1992 or Saudi Arabia in 1992. Contrasted with these are, for example, England, France, Australia, and the United States—where human rights have an extraordinarily large and growing voice in public affairs. The abortion conflict in the United States of America is a typical example of freedom from state control: to decide whether or not a person's private decision shall stand on whether to abort or not. Central is the idea of limit to government. Where freedom from the state has particular strength, as it does in the United States, the conflict of those who want to channel the abortion decision compared with those who want to have government control personal human autonomy is self-evident. Privacy prevails over state control that is seen to be limited—beyond its sphere of competence. Other decisions, such as what clothes to wear, how to be educated, what religion to profess, whether to have children or not, how to educate children, what to eat, and when to sleep are a wide range of comparable decisions almost always beyond government competence. One could speculate easily that many more such decisions are private than public. Some would call these artistic liberty, freedom of speech, freedom of association and freedom of religion, the core of the First Amendment (the written evidence that marks the beginning of a *vast* sea of human rights into which a few governments have been created and thrust by will of the people). While Karl Marx and others dreamed of the "withering away of the state," by great contrast in the United States the state is told—that is, state, local and federal governments are ordered by judges—to keep their noses out of people's businesses and lives. This key value of privacy is respected in the United States—widely respected and maintained. Freedom from the snoop is valued. This creates enormous tension with the state agents who wish to invade personal inner liberty. The power of personal inner liberty is so valuable that it is sought to protect the property of the Fortune 500—wrongly appropriated in such a case—misused by them.

The advocates of religious freedom, free enterprise, capitalism, and private property and privacy particularly are enamored with privacy in this context; they want maximum freedom from state regulation and control. They want it inside nations and among nations. Consider this, the grand global strategy of such advocates is to create a single European market and a single North American market where national constraints dissolve in the name of "free trade." The national constraints are merely the laws of states. The details of this problem are spelled out in Chapter 6.

To recapitulate, freedom is structured into national freedom, freedom within a state and freedom from a state. Laws of international and domestic scope treat every one of these topics in great depth in some nations. But beyond laws, a need for greater authority and order, a need to protect private property, a need to provide justice, a need to achieve more equality among citizens, and a need to promote and protect privacy (personal autonomy from state and corporate interference) each of these significant values restrict someone in a society in different ways and in different degrees over time. Freedom is expanded for some so that others will have lesser freedom. And in some cases, national freedom when threatened may require the stringency of warlike action inside a state—price and commodity control, strict regulation of the entire economy. John Kenneth Galbraith the economist and author was the czar of the American economy during World War II. Food-rationing stamps during World War II are clear evidence that in an era of total war, even food regardless of our freedom to eat what we choose, is rationed. The freedom within the state is powerful; the freedom from the state is overpowering unless one does not feel like eating in times of global war.

At the outset of this book, the question was offered: Is liberty a contingent value and not preeminent? To answer this question with transformed freedom and the interplay with other contingent values, one would think the obvious answer would be a flat *no*, liberty is not preeminent, it is a contingent value. It all depends upon the circumstances, which if serious enough may overweigh a national predisposition toward freedom. But I think there is such a powerful sentiment behind all three aspects of freedom that just as often liberty defeats other important values. If we knew more, it would be easier to give a flat answer one way or another to the question above. In the next chapter, there is a chance to examine more circumstances that have a bearing on national freedom, freedom within a state and freedom from a state. Contingency certainly is present in the examples considered. No absolutes exist except perhaps for slavery and torture in America.

Chapter 6

Transformed Freedom: Application of Important Conclusions and New Beginnings for the American Dream of Freedom

This chapter focuses on the application of the new transformed freedom to the range of problems found in Chapters 1 to 4 that were characterized as either too many or too few freedoms. Some new problems will be analyzed as well. This application should answer the question: Does the basic contradiction of too many or too few freedoms become dissolved by the transformation of the idea of freedom suggested in Chapter 5? Can we see things more clearly in relation to all three aspects of freedom? To think about it in a schematic manner, the three basic aspects of freedom—national freedom, freedom within a state and freedom from a state—are each shaped in their own way by the basic contingent values of authority, property, equality, justice and privacy. This contingent and divergent nature of liberty was explained in Chapter 5. As we examine each aspect of freedom it becomes clear that our attention would be ordered in a different way for national freedom—true national autonomy—than it would be for freedom within a state where federalism and separation of powers would be among the important critical freedom issues. And these two major aspects are further differentiated from the third aspect of freedom—freedom from a state or one's inner liberty. It all depends.

IT ALL DEPENDS

Depending upon the type of freedom and upon the contingent nonfreedom values, depending upon the example given, and depending upon the place and time when something must be decided, there is a significant difference in these aspects of freedom that can be readily grasped. Contingency seems to be pervasive.

In other words, for example, if one is concerned about foreign or alien acquisition of high technology from American corporations in the United States as Susan and Martin Tolchin clearly are concerned in *Selling Our Security* (1992), then you think of the national freedom and autonomy at stake. Then you think of the relationship of corporations to a nation and you ask whether these corporations have too much freedom to dispose of their assets in a capitalistic free enterprise economy. Then you ask—is it fair to the nation—where the corporation may have received large sums of money in grants and tax subsidies for research and development that is then acquired by a foreign corporation with no significant approval or clearance by national authorities?[1] Without some form of governmental clearance, national assets and boundaries are meaningless or are becoming that way rapidly. We shall examine this issue more fully later in this chapter.

When the issue is freedom from a state—the condition of the inner liberty of a woman who wants to have an abortion is seen in the context of the limits to state authority or in a balance in the state authority to achieve justice for mother, father, child, siblings and others and to respect the privacy and autonomy of a woman. The essential question is how to draw that practical line between what is the private domain of each person and what is the shared individual-community concern or domain. In a nation with a powerful tradition of individualism, the way the line is drawn is significant to a lot of people as a future rule in their own lives. A better definition of liberty does not make this line-drawing much easier, but it does clarify wonderfully, what part of freedom is of concern and what contingent values—whether authority, property, equality, justice or privacy—are at stake and will somehow or other channel the nature of the freedom exercised in a particular area. We draw closer to the truth about liberty.

Since each application in this chapter depends upon a host of contingent factors, the application of the ideas of transformed freedom requires a renewal of thinking about liberty. Let us next give consideration to the way historians of liberty thought about liberty in an international and a national sense.

A PERSPECTIVE OF HISTORIANS ON FREEDOM APPLICATIONS

Many think Americans are too ahistorical or not interested in their past. This is not actually true when it comes to freedom. Let us examine prime examples.

Herbert Joseph Muller, a scholar of the idea of freedom who wrote twelve books on a variety of subjects, devoted at least five of them to the subject of freedom. Most noted for *The Loom of History* (1958), he also wrote *The Issues of Freedom* (1960), *Freedom in the Ancient World* (1961), *Freedom in the Western World* (1963), *Religion and Freedom in the Modern World* (1963) and *Freedom in the Modern World* (1966).[2] A rich mother lode of material and analysis spanning all of Western Civilization, Muller's work offers a consistent, single human perspective in well over a thousand pages. I started with this scholar's perspective and examined it a quarter century later because it offered a starting point of substance and unqualified merit.

First, Muller's definition of freedom was consciously kept understandable. "The condition of being able to choose and carry out purposes" was how he defined freedom. He was committed to the principles of John Stuart Mill stated in *On Liberty* (1859). Freedom and the state, he explained, expanded to cover issues of freedom in the society—especially political freedom in the 19th and 20th centuries as compared with earlier centuries. The impact of the Industrial Revolution was to complicate understanding of freedom as was the rise of modern science and technology. He asked in 1966, "Are Americans freer in this century than they were at the beginning of the preceding one? Today [more] than a generation ago? The usual answer is that they are less free. The obvious answer seems to me Yes and No, in various ways."[3] The complications for an historian are many, but he offered a perspective with about a dozen significant events bearing on the state of freedom one way or another in America. In the twenty years from the end of World War II, 1946 to 1966, these are the events significant to Muller:

- Dawn of the Atomic Age
- Emergence of Soviet Union and spread of Communism
- Establishment of United Nations and many new nations
- Revolt of nonwestern world, end of colonialism
- Conquest of space and moon project
- Discovery of genetic codes
- Knowledge explosion in science
- Education explosion in colleges and universities
- Growth of an affluent society
- Dawn of automation and computers
- Development of electronics, television, supersonic planes, intercontinental missiles, and so forth.[4]

Almost seeing the future, Muller wrote in 1966: "Nevertheless, we still have reason to hope that the Cold War will remain a substitute instead of a preparation for a hideous total war."[5]

So far, he guessed right on this future. In an epilogue on the twenty-year period after World War II, Muller quietly and prophetically examined the state of American society noting the factors including those mentioned just above. In 1966 he said that American affluence:

Exasperated the ugliest problem of the day, the long overdue revolt of the Negro. It will no longer do merely to give Negroes their civil rights, which they already enjoy in the North: the most difficult task is economic—to give them something like equality of opportunity.[6]

Muller asked whether self-hood is doomed by the nature of an affluent mass society and suggested that he discounted such alarms being sounded then. Thirteen years later, Christopher Lasch wrote *The Culture of Narcissism* (1979) that offers a different view.

While not doing justice to Muller's body of work, I note that Muller found exceptional energy and creativity to be by-products of western traditions of individualism. The society allowed people to speak out and they did; it was an open society in 1966 in terms of politics, intellectual pursuits, religious or nonreligious elements of spirituality, but tending to regimentation and standardization in many aspects of life. This perspective of Muller was a wholesome, educated, broad and sophisticated view of America in 1966 and the state of freedom then being enjoyed.

Since that time, from 1966 to 1992, we have had the Korean, Vietnam and Persian Gulf Wars, a president nearly impeached, a vast growth in the Civil Rights movement, a rebirth of equal rights movements for women called a feminist movement, and a stirring by formerly silent groups such as homosexuals, students, prisoners, mental patients, disabled persons and others. The end of the Cold War, the momentous change in the former Soviet Union and other eastern bloc nations still is ringing in our ears and being felt in our psyches.

By 1992, enforced child labor, debt bondage and traditional chattel slavery reemerged across India, Africa, Asia and the Middle East. The fact that forms of slavery exist today is indicative of the persistence of the problem generation after generation anywhere on the globe. Freedom is a struggle, not a final resting place.

When the United States reached its Constitutional 200th birthday in 1987 and when the Bill of Rights reached 200 years of age in 1991, the outpouring of literature about the American experience with, and experimentation with, freedom became a magnificent brisk industry of new literature about America. To close this introductory, historical perspective on American freedom, I chose another widely known historian author, James MacGregor Burns, an eminent scholar and one of America's prominent biographers of Franklin Delano Roosevelt and John F. Kennedy. His historical work anticipated the 200-year old celebrations of the United States.

Three books by James MacGregor Burns deserve special attention. In *The Vineyard of Liberty* (1982) the period from shaping the constitution of the United States in the 1780s to 1863 when Lincoln signed the Emancipation Proclamation, Burns offers an extraordinarily detailed historical insight. Burns noted the "Grandest question of them all—the extent to which government should interfere with some persons' liberties in order to grant them and other persons more liberty and equality.[7] The stream of new slaves and the politics of slavery hung like a brooding storm until April 12, 1861, when the shelling of Fort Sumter in the narrows of Charleston Harbor, marked the start of the Civil War. By 1865 the war was over; Lincoln had been assassinated and 650,000 lay dead from war in a reunited America.

The second book, *The Workshop of Democracy* (1985), Burns examined the seven decades from the Emancipation Proclamation in 1863 through World War I and the Great Depression. Here the national economic and social transformation is a dominant theme. Finally, in a third book, *The Crosswinds of Freedom* (1989), Burns asked explicitly what kind of freedom, what strategies of freedom, and what liberation struggles fit into the last five and a half decades of American history? He ended with a question that addressed whether there is a rebirth of freedom. Burns looked back over 200 years of the "American experiment" and saw planned experiences, such as the constitution and space exploration, the unplanned Civil War butchery, and forty other similar facets. Burns was clear—the grand experiment of true magnificence was to expand individual liberty and real equality of opportunity found in American freedom. Burns wrote in 1989, "This experiment was called Freedom, combining as it did liberty and equality."[8] He followed with sage advice on the future of the experiment in the United States.

The historian's perspective of Herbert Joseph Muller and James MacGregor Burns is very important to grasp because little or no under-standing of American freedom and freedom elsewhere is possible without this basic knowledge. It provides what Charles Taylor described as the moral horizon for action. The foundation or groundwork found in books like these and many others are a definition of the American community—a national and a global community that deserves greater attention; for it is within a common history that one can see the genuine significance of freedom to mankind writ large. New scholarship is advancing insights into freedom through the work of Orlando Patterson, Michael Kammen and Harold Berman. Their books are respectively titled: *Freedom: Freedom in the Making of Western Cultures* (1991); *Spheres of Liberty: Changing Perceptions of Liberty in American Culture* (1986) and *Law and Revolution: The Transformation of the Western Legal Tradition* (1983). This interpretive work is of the kind that enriches and satisfies curiosity while stimulating one to examine the issues further. I have precisely identified and commented on historical perspective in the study of freedom because this discipline will never advance without significant attention being paid to its history in many ways. While not exclusively, I have drawn heavily on their understanding and knowledge of freedom to formulate my concepts of freedom.

FREEDOM APPLICATIONS

The aim of the next major part of this chapter is to apply the transformed idea of freedom to specific problems and issues mentioned before in previous chapters. The three major parts of freedom—national freedom, freedom within a state and freedom from a state—each have significant issues of freedom that are affected in different ways by other values or contingencies—authority, property, equality, justice and privacy. It is worth observing that national freedom waxes and wanes depending upon the nation, the time and the circumstances, variables that profoundly affect the position of a nation in the world community. Nations being born or breaking apart differ in their national freedom from nations having a stable existence over long periods of time. Freedom within a nation or state ranges from tyrannical to open society in basic condition. Here too, the state of the society is a significant variable. Finally, freedom from a state or nation or society—inner liberty—is a creature of extraordinary attention in America, even more than freedom within the nation. Let us proceed with the application, keeping the perspective of a historian constantly in mind.

PART I. NATIONAL FREEDOM—TRUE NATIONAL AUTONOMY IN A GLOBAL SOCIETY

Nationalism is a child of freedom, but it can happen that the child kills its mother.[9]

The oldest aspect of freedom is freedom of a community from external or alien domination or despotism. Perhaps every nation that exists today in its own history has at one time or another faced what the ancient Greeks called a threat to *autonomia*, a natural right to live in a state with laws of its own choosing. In such a state or nation, one experiences the meaning of national freedom. There is little doubt that a clear trend exists in this field of freedom. From 1946 to 1993, the original UN members have increased from 49 to 178, a growth of 129 nations or well over 200 percent in a quarter century. Spurts of nation creation were in 1955, 1960 and 1992. The continual pressure to create new nations illustrates better than anything the truth that external liberty of a state is a great motivator to groups of people across the globe. And, this fact of nationhood growth shows how

Ehrenberg's belief is accurate, "people would rather have self-government, with all its difficulties and uncertainties, than live under foreign rule no matter how well-meaning." The end of colonialism is perfect evidence of this truth. The freedom from external domination does *not* assure that a dictator or despot may not rule the nation in its interior activities. Neither does it guarantee that the rule will or will not be democratic.[10]

Obviously, nations differ in their size, strength and capacity to defend themselves, which led, more than 2,500 years ago in Greece to leagues of city-states and to alliances for self-protection from those who wanted to conquer the world and expand their sphere of influence. Think of Athens and Sparta. Then, alliances of nations fought alliances of nations out of a fear of loss of self-governance liberty. This behavior is not a changing condition of mankind. It goes back at least 5,000 years. A belief in liberty for one's own state would not exclude automatically a will to dominate and tyrannize other nations.

Ehrenberg suggested that all the nation building of the last five decades offers great opportunities and great dangers to both the individual nation and to all 178 nations in the UN. Considering national freedom as a separate facet of freedom, in general, we must, in this analytical framework, ask ourselves questions about conditions or contingencies that affect this type of freedom. War, either civil or against external enemies, is a major circumstance that has a direct and visible impact on freedom for the nation among nations and freedom inside the nation at war.

Nuremberg War Crime Trials

The first illustration is from the Nuremberg war crime trials following World War II. The value of justice constrains the acts of combatants in fighting—it constrains national freedom to do anything one pleases during war. Wilhelm Keitel, one of the Nazis tried in the Nuremberg war crime trials in 1946, stated in his last words at the end of the trials:

It is tragic to have to realize that the best I had to give as a soldier, obedience and loyalty, was exploited for purposes that could not be recognized at the time, and that I did not see that there is a limit even for a soldier's performance of his duty. THAT IS MY FATE.[11]

Keitel was judged, sentenced to death and was hanged along with nine others. In his cell, Herman Goering committed suicide with a poison capsule. Without a doubt, national freedom has limits that the Nuremberg Trials did assert against the remaining, responsible Nazi leaders in 1946. The key element of justice was brought to bear by the victors after the war.

Nothing could be said to embellish the power of justice to make national freedom a conditional or contingent value in these circumstances. Freedom of a nation does not justify an Auschwitz concentration camp or gross inhumanity to Germans and non-Germans, Jewish and non-Jewish, all caught up in the chaotic madness of Hitler's Germany in World War II. The Nuremberg war crime trials establish this barrier to total national freedom, hopefully for all time. Recent events in former Yugoslavia may crush this hope of a half century.

Reflections of Albert Camus on Quarter Truth of Liberty

Moral passion stirs us in powerful ways—it moves our spirit. In a strange way, the French author Albert Camus, who won the Nobel Prize for literature in 1957 and who died too early in life in 1964, deeply effects some of us today. It is true in my case of writing about liberty, and it is true of William Styron, an American novelist. Camus's influence is clear in Styron's moving self-revelation of deep personal depression in *Darkness Visible*. Camus wrote about suicide in *The Myth of Sisyphus*. When struggling with his own possible suicide, Styron said of Camus's message of the triumph of life over death "in the absence of hope we must still struggle to survive, and so we do—by the skin of our teeth." [12] Styron saw Camus as a writer who weds moral passion "to a style of great beauty and whose unblinking vision is capable of frightening the soul to its marrow." [13] These are things of the spirit.

As I mentioned previously, *The Plague* by Camus is an arresting and frightening novel that stimulated my interest in Camus. But more than this work, far more, is the 1961 collection of writings titled *Resistance, Rebellion and Death*.[14] It is a collection of Camus' writings. In parts titled *The Letters to a German Friend* and in *The Liberation of Paris*, Camus explained the nature of the French spirit that survived during Nazi occupation in 1940-1945. Camus wrote letters to a fictional friend, a German (Nazi), and in *The Fourth Letter* he said:

You supposed that . . . the only values were those of the animal world . . . violence and cunning. . . . You concluded that man was negligible and . . . his soul could be killed, that in the maddest of histories the only pursuit for the individual was the adventure of power and his only morality, the realism of conquests.[15]

Camus was disgusted with his Nazi captors. Nazi Germans trampled civilization. The cruel injustice of Nazi occupation of France began to lift on August 24, 1944, when Camus described the city of Paris with bombers, snipers and fires burning in the City of Light:

Bursting with all the fires of hope and suffering the flame of lucid courage and all the glow, not only of liberation, but of tomorrow's liberty.[16]

By August 25, 1944, the bullets of freedom whistled through the city; truth and justice finally prevailed after a miserably brutal and tortured period of years—at a great price of blood and dead French men, women and children. Camus said that man's greatness lies in the decision to be stronger than his condition—without revenge or spite—to achieve justice. These moving reflections set the tone and background in an even more profound revelation of Camus to appear in the part titled: *The Wager of our Generation,* an interview of Camus in October 1957 presented in *Resistance, Rebellion and Death.* A question asked of Camus was this:

The most serious one is a problem for all men: in all the struggles dividing the world today, must we really be willing to forget all that is bad on one side to fight what is worse on the other? [17]

Camus replied:

Before he died in combat in the last war, Richard Hilary found the phrase that sums up this dilemma: "WE ARE FIGHTING A LIE IN THE NAME OF A HALF TRUTH." He thought he was expressing a very pessimistic idea. *But one may even have to fight a lie in the name of a quarter-truth.* (Emphasis added). This is our situation at present. However, the quarter-truth contained in Western society is called liberty. And liberty is the way, and the only way, of perfectibility. Without liberty heavy industry can be perfected, but not justice or truth. Our most recent history, from Berlin to Budapest, ought to convince us of this. In any case, it is the reason for my choice. I have said in this very place that none of the evils totalitarianism claims to remedy is worse than totalitarianism itself. I have not changed my mind. On the contrary, after twenty years of our harsh history, during which I have tried to accept every experience it offered, liberty ultimately seems to me, for societies and for individuals, for labor and for culture, the supreme good that governs all others.[18]

For Camus and for others, that powerful statement seems to be a good place to start thinking about liberty and its global importance as a potential supreme good. Is liberty a supreme good to reach justice and truth? Is liberty not in conflict with, but in support of justice and truth? Should liberty and justice together with truth be harnessed to produce a society of greater perfection?

Is liberty the universal supreme good that governs all others? Or is liberty contingent? Orlando Patterson assumed that freedom is a supreme good in his 1991 book, *Freedom.* Yet this view can be challenged and supported. Must we fight lies in the name, not of full truth, nor half-truths, but in the name of quarter truths? Is this the one truth about liberty even today? Is liberty the only way to perfectibility? In all of these profound questions, or conclusions, if you prefer, Camus's wisdom rings out too clearly to ignore. What Camus said about liberty seems to be posed as a universal truth. But to fight such a conclusion Walter Lippmann would have looked for word "qualifiers" and "weasel" words to create exceptions for universals.[19] Life without liberty may not be worth living, or as Patrick Henry, the great Virginian and American Revolutionary leader, said: "Give me liberty or give me death." Life may be a continual struggle to reassert human liberty in the face of injustice and lies, and even in the absence of bare hope of decent existence during the Nazi occupation. The condition of despairing national hope faced Camus and other French men and women.

There may be no better place to begin thinking about liberty than to take observations and ideas of Camus to heart and consider the man who intelligently expressed these ideas—not only through the tough times of World War II, but through the Cold War that followed. His condition was tragedy heaped upon hopelessness in the Cold War. National freedom was obliterated. Only now in the 1990s does the Cold War thaw and melt away, but the chill of nuclear harm lies all around two huge continents and over and under the world's oceans. United States and Russian submarines still may collide accidentally beneath polar icecaps. The biblical echoes of "wars" and rumors of wars have not ceased. The nuclear threat—the true lack of hope—remains, but those weakened by this struggle should not whine about the condition. Liberty in the form of national freedom is defended in the United States and Europe; liberty lies dormant in many places on the globe, but where liberty now begins to light up anew is in Eastern Europe and the former Soviet Union. Eduard Shevardnaze in *The Future Belongs to Freedom* (1991) reflects on this idea.

Camus probably would revel at the tenacity of the truth of liberty (a quarter truth) to survive during so long a cold war—once again proving that liberty quite possibly may be the supreme good of Camus that guides and energizes all other values. However, wanting to believe that this is so does not make it true. Thus, the long search, a personal search of mine was started, inflamed and motivated by the potential for truth—full truth—that lies within Albert Camus's brilliant observations about liberty. And I take Camus to mean by liberty in this context national freedom, the ancient Greek *autonomia*. Nothing so vivid and brief is written about liberty, nothing so conclusive sounding is said about liberty compared with that explained by Camus during the 1957 interview mentioned above. There are, however, a wide range of comparably beautiful and thoughtful observations about the meaning of liberty from a diverse group of writers across the world. Each fruitful observation is similar to a facet of a diamond that sparkles in the sunlight. Together, these facets of liberty most vividly illustrate the profound and persistent nature of liberty in Western Civilization. And there are falsehoods about liberty that need exposure. I think it should be getting clearer just what such a falsehood could be.

American Judge Learned Hand—1945 Liberty Defined

Because the American legal profession defends human liberty by observing the Bill of Rights, it seems appropriate to remember Judge Learned Hand, a federal United States Judge who spoke to a group of citizens at a naturalization hearing and public gathering on May 21, 1944, in Central Park in New York City. This speech has justly become famous. Just as Camus saw liberty in national freedom emerging in Paris during 1944 from World War II and from ending of the Nazi occupation in Europe, Judge Learned Hand—thousands of miles away in New York City—saw liberty as national freedom emerging in Hand's own inimitable way. At almost the same time as Camus, an American Judge spoke to immigrants. The voices of Camus and Hand ring out loudly, waiting to be reheard by new generations who are puzzled about their liberty.

Judge Learned Hand asked in this brief but famous speech in Central Park:

What do we mean when we say that first of all we seek liberty? I often wonder whether we do not rest our hopes too much upon constitutions, upon laws and upon courts. These are false hopes; believe me, these are false hopes. Liberty lies in the hearts of men and women; when it dies there, no constitution, no law, no court can save it; no constitution, no law, no court can even do much to help it. While it lies there it needs no constitution, no law, no court to save it. And what is this liberty which must lie in the hearts of men and women? It is not the ruthless, the unbridled will; it is not freedom to do as one likes. This is a denial of liberty, and leads straight to its overthrow. A society in which men recognize no check upon their freedom soon becomes a society where freedom is the possession of only a savage few; as we have learned to our sorrow.

What then is the spirit of liberty? I cannot define it; I can only tell you my own faith. The spirit of liberty is
- the spirit which is not too sure that it is right
- the spirit of liberty is the spirit which seeks to understand the minds of other men and women
- the spirit of liberty is the spirit which weighs their interests alongside its own without bias
- the spirit of liberty remembers that not even a sparrow falls to earth unheeded
- the spirit of liberty is the spirit of Him who, near two thousand years ago, taught mankind that lesson it has never learned, but has never quite forgotten;

that there may be a kingdom where the least shall be heard and considered side by side with the greatest (emphasis added).[20]

There is no reasonable way to ignore the spirit of liberty defined by Judge Hand in his splendid faith that the spirit of liberty:

1. Is not too sure that it is right (self-skeptical)
2. Seeks to understand the needs of others (outward focusing)
3. Weighs interest of others alongside of oneself without bias (impartial in nature)
4. Remembers the weak and humble (treats all with equality and charity)

Judge Hand was reflecting upon a potential meaning of national freedom given the circumstances of his speech. To emphasize contrasting views of national freedom, these traits of liberty are not arrogantly cocky and self-assured; they are not bull-headed and narrow-minded or self-centered; they are not biased towards oneself; and they express charity toward the meek and humble in society. National freedom lacks what the Greeks call *hubris*, or insolent arrogance, and shines with *sophrosyne*, or moderation. These are not traits of the Nazi Germans who were vain, self-centered, arrogant, demonic, conquering masters of the human race. Much the same could be said of Imperial Japan in its military vanities and Kamikaze pursuits, and the same is true of Mussolini's Italians. The spirit of liberty is a compassionate and endearing human quality if we think of it the way Judge Hand thought. This visage of liberty could justify calling it the supreme good that Camus found. In fact, Camus justified French indecision at the beginning of Nazi occupation because his countrymen needed to think through what was right, what the Nazis stood for, what the French wanted without spite or revenge, and how the Nazi's treated the weak and humble. The questions were answered by the French resistance, an underground fight against Nazis and their French sympathizers.

To open this analysis of national freedom with the thinking of two extraordinary people—American judge Learned Hand and a famous Nobel Prize winning Frenchman of letters, Albert Camus—suggests an important feature of national freedom. This freedom is shared by different nations in the Western world when fighting for national freedom or liberty in 1944 was the supreme preoccupation of the living in Europe, Asia and America and across the globe. Also, it was the dawn of the atomic age and nuclear warfare by 1945. A half century later, the world has turned many times, but the quarter truth of liberty in the minds of Hand and Camus remains clearly visible before us—a lasting idea of supreme merit. It deserves much greater attention today so that we grasp the truth about national liberty—even a quarter truth.

Liberty, truth and justice mingle in mutual reflection upon one another in these perspectives. Other significant human values according to Hand and Camus come into play as well such as curiosity, humility, compassion for the weak and humble, and generosity of spirit. Liberty is a spiritual, and therefore, an intangible element of human nature, but it is just as real as any other aspect of nature. Neither Albert Camus nor Judge Learned Hand were writing about fictional liberty. The stresses of 1944 in World War II on the future of Western Civilization followed by a Cold War energized some thoughtful people to reflect on the truth, expressing what is real about liberty. Mankind is blessed that it is not tested every year as severely as in 1944. But we benefit by listening to the thoughtful in times of acute, global tragedy, about what liberty meant to them, what liberty should and could mean as an ideal of national freedom.

Freedom for Citizen Fortune 500 Corporations and Citizen Multinational Corporations

There is an aspect of national freedom in which the thunder of the coming storm is rumbling louder and louder. One can trace over a hundred years of gathering storm clouds that may dump their floods of trouble on America before the start of the 21st century. I mean the trouble caused by the freedom of the nearly stateless giant corporations to act in the United States and elsewhere just as a human being citizen may act without any of the attributes of being a human. And then giant corporations pretend that a philosophy of commercial free enterprise authorizes corporate global sovereignty. No death, omnipresence in 50 states and 100 nations, massive financial resources, wedding of bureaucracy and technology with modern mass communication—these attributes define corporate giants. In a word, POWER. These are just some of the nonhuman traits of what is called strangely a corporate person or citizen in America. For example, Coca Cola, General Motors, Exxon and Ford, do they claim rights under the Bill of Rights for people? Yes! Are these companies just ordinary plain folks, or are they not folks at all to which the citizenship rights of human beings should not attach? How free should corporate giants be allowed to be? Are corporate giants not private corporations, but public corporations deeply colored by size alone?

What I propose is to examine aspects of the last 100 years of experience with major American corporations. This period covers the robber baron era and Sherman Antitrust Act of 1890 to control big monopolizing business to the present time. This is a focus on the free, but definitely darker, illegal and corrupt side of the American business and economy. This history is the rationale for regulation of business. The background will enable you to see how national freedom, national and popular sovereignty, is being challenged and disrupted seriously by multinational businesses that span nations, but ultimately depend upon specific nations to keep the peace with armies, to protect corporate plants, property, patents and contracts, and to foster a favorable business climate while pleading with governments to tax the companies minimally. This discussion is not intended to be corporation bashing, and it is not intended to be protectionist fear of foreign competition. Instead, the analysis portrays the true state of affairs in America with regard to national freedom for nations living with multinational corporations of the ilk of the Bank of Credit and Commerce International (BCCI). Peter Truell and Larry Gurwin in *False Profits* (1992) document the world's most corrupt financial empire, BCCI. This topic is merely an illustration of how multinational corporate freedom must be guided by equally powerful national and state sovereign authority, property protections, equality of treatment, considerations of justice and respect for privacy. These channeling values reveal starkly how outrageous are some of the claims of freedom by modern corporate America. These claims of corporate sovereignty threaten national sovereignty as it has never been experienced before.

There is justification for attention to national freedom expressed by social critics who deserve our attention. Freedom in America—its general condition in the last few decades is a subject seriously examined by three exceptional writers with diverse backgrounds and perspectives on America. They are not peas in a pod. They think brilliantly as well. William Greider's views are mentioned here briefly and are examined more thoroughly later in Chapter 6. The editor of *Harper's Magazine*, Lewis Lapham, is concerned for the future of democracy and freedom and the well-known trial attorney and author from Wyoming, Gerry Spence, shares that concern. Both in 1993 offered parallel expressions indicting corporate American businesses for excessive political, economic and social intervention and control of the people of the nation—stifling the sovereignty and freedoms of the people of the United States. These are serious indictments of big business "free enterprise" philosophy and the corresponding corrosive social action.

William Greider asked a basic question about freedom in America in the title to his best-selling 1992 work: *Who Will Tell the People? The Betrayal of American Democracy*. The book provides examples of the pathetic ways that ordinary people try to speak to power. It suggests failure in the mediating voices of political parties and the "rancid populism" of the Republican party, and it highlights the failure of the news media and the inept mass media's one-way channel of communication that Greider called mindlessly destructive. And Greider had a very special place for General Electric which he labeled *Citizen GE* as if he were speaking of Citizen Kane.

This giant corporation is a growing threat to freedom and democracy in America in his view. Greider noted the destabilizing of political processes in America since the ending of the Cold War, and he thought that soulless transnational American and other corporations harbor closet dictators. There was evidence in the secret negotiation process for treaties that the public has not one bit of business in such business. People were insulted by not even being consulted by their leaders before a "solution" was foisted on them in the savings and loan scandal immediately after the election of President Bush. The same feeling surrounds the General Agreement on Tariffs and Trade (GATT) and North American Free Trade Agreement (NAFTA) treaties schemed out in private. The trust of citizens in both government and business plunges to new lows while betrayal of their interests was discovered too late by the people. This was and is a condition identified by Greider that is darkly ominous and foreboding for the future of the nation and its freedoms.

Lewis H. Lapham in *The Wish for Kings - Democracy at Bay*, published 1993, offered much evidence over a long time in America and it offered such cogent, well-crafted arguments that the book left little doubt that we, the American public, yearn for a king to simplify public life. And no one could do justice to Lapham's description of the "courtier spirit"—the boot-licking cowardly spirit in business, government, academia, and elsewhere. As he suggested, even many of our presidents have an odor of ancient regality in their own words and actions. And Lapham asks why H. Ross Perot got nineteen million votes in 1992 for President of the United States. The answer is simple—some of us yearn for an autocrat. The spirit is abroad in the land, some nineteen-million strong—straight out of the military-industrial complex and technocracy spawned by the trillions of dollars paid by the "owners of America" in taxes and debts of the United States government. Perot was one of the extraordinary winners in the transfer of wealth.

Lapham explains that the ruling oligarchy in America is a government of the rich, by the rich and for the rich. I would call it a plutocracy. The oligarchy is small in number of people, "populist billionaires" exist in its midst, and it controls the nation, especially the many courtiers in service to it. Lapham tells us that the courtier spirit consists in telling welcome lies —denying and distorting the truth. Weird ideas, like "plausible deniability," crop up in such craven situations. Flattering and fawning have their place in the court. The comforts of cartels and monopolies are extolled. The press and news media are corporate-owned and are not free to write or speak the truth if it conflicts with the master's wish. "Suck-up" coverage, a new term for me, expressed what some of the press and media do for their daily bread.

Lapham said, "If we wish to live in a state of freedom, then we must accustom ourselves to the shadows on the walls and wind in the trees."[21] Permanent uncertainty, or a republic if you have the "guts" to keep it and other admonitions were made by him. Lapham echoes Greider when he states "The post-Cold War world begins to look like medieval Europe."[22] The oligarchies of America, Germany, Mexico and Japan resemble each other more than they do the citizens of their respective nations. Lapham said that democracy and freedom are not in the future of a people who are "seeking to make peace with anybody who will promise them another twenty minutes of life, liberty and the pursuit of happiness."[23] This punch line resembles the quotation of John Stuart Mill that opened this book. Barbarians will take over the oligarchies not fit to survive.

The third important voice, that of Gerry Spence, the famous writer and trial attorney from Jackson Hole, Wyoming, sprang forth in 1993 when he offered *From Freedom to Slavery: The Rebirth of Tyranny in America.* St. Martin's Press published this book that slices deep into corporate America and particularly the insurance industry. Americans must, according to Spence, wake up to their own enslavement by television, by modern technology, by corporate giants and their oligarchies, and soon end the illusion of freedom that is fed to them. "The brainwashing has dehumanized us. It has left us comporting ourselves like lumpen slobs drooling at the trough where we are slopped like anthromorphic hogs with the vacuous fare corporate America throws at us." [24]

Spence in his lawsuits has fought corporate America and the giant federal agencies so that he knows whereof he speaks when he decides to speak to power. Spence concludes his masterful essays this way:

For more than two hundred years, like evil termites, disenfranchising ideas have gnawed away at the supporting timbers in American democracy. From the beginning, women have been vassalized. So have minorities. So have workers and artists and lovers of the earth. Far more deracinating is the historic progression in America that finds living people governed by non-living corporations, that in a democracy nonliving corporations should own our legislatures, buy our presidents, select our judges, possess our airways, pollute our rivers, foul our oceans, and poison our skies.[25]

One may disagree with Spence's evidence and analysis, powerful as it is, but adding this voice to those of Greider and Lapham, each from such a unique, well-educated and respected perspective, I must conclude that we are now witnessing in America a breakthrough and rebirth of exceptional and powerful political, social and economic dissent. This dissent premises human freedom and democracy to be worthwhile for the bulk of humanity, not just for the "happy few" that Lapham mentions. These American voices are directed towards problems of concern to everyone. They are clear voices, not bellowings and rantings at the fringe of the herd. In these circumstances the definition of freedom becomes that much more significant to help us sustain reasoned discourse about power, wealth and rights and their recognition and distribution in America.

In several of the preceding chapters, there were references to the too-free corporate chief executives of some Fortune 500 and other major corporations. The problem of freedom—national freedom of the United States government with respect to other nations and fifty states, private institutions and private organizations—is basically a question of sovereignty. As Michael Kammen articulated it, "Sovereignty and liberty have long been vital concepts in the continuum of human perceptions concerning the nature of political authority and the quest for freedom." [26] Who governs is very important. Who is the ultimate superior sovereign power of America? In this context, since it is not a nation or state, can a multinational corporation serve two masters at the same time? Can a modern American multinational corporation divide its loyalties, being equally loyal to all the nations and various states in the United States where it does business? Can a multinational corporation be loyal to the country and loyal to its owners (stockholders) and managers? Are dual loyalties, like dual citizenship to state and nation, to family and community, to business and to the community such a common thing that there is no problem of divided loyalty of multinational corporations to fifty nations in which they simultaneously do business? It takes no expertise at the end of the 20th century, when a united European economy and large trading blocks of nations are a distinct probability, to see vividly the corporate international penetration of foreign and domestic markets to the point where apologists for the global economy argue openly that "You just cannot tell where an automobile is made." "You cannot tell where the European Airbus is made." Rules of origin in trade agreements counteract this. It is as if this confusion is of no consequence in human affairs; as if a nation and its fundamental sovereignty are unimportant in United Nations relationships, in war, taxation, border control, immigration or domestic and foreign trade. And, it is as if labor should not care where things are made; that manufacturing can move anywhere on earth that pleases it and it alone. The mix of internal and external is purposely becoming a genuinely complex issue. Furthermore, it takes no special expertise, either economic or political, to ask questions about control of major domestic industries in time of war. What if the government of the United States wished to command all of the United States airline companies to serve its needs in time of war, say a Desert Storm War, when this in fact happened? But suppose some other nation or foreign multinational corporation owned the airline and disagreed about the war? These questions we will tackle shortly.

Corporate Sovereignty

If an American airline company is purchased by a foreign carrier, say for example, British Airways Corporation buys a controlling share of USAir, can it be asked fairly by what right does the government of the United States have the power and authority to prohibit a foreign entity from controlling a United States airline? After all, in the preemption of state power, the United States government does the same thing to the fifty states in the United States. Does sovereignty of a nation (in this case the United States government) give way logically to foreign treaties, GATT Agreements, to multinational CEOs and their global markets and marketers and let them—those in the market—decide for themselves unilaterally how to structure their international business and economic arrangements? Does wartime power become irrelevant? Milton Friedman in *Capitalism and Freedom* (1982 edition) sees detailed regulation of industries, especially transport industries without justification based on the negligible role he assigns to government. The blindness of Friedman, who would sacrifice national sovereignty, is obvious.

Yet, such a fight between five carriers—Delta, American, United, British Airways and USAir—reached a crisis stage. That is, full-page advertisements in major newspapers by the three carriers (Delta, American and United) hit the press in late 1992 seriously questioning the "deal" of a foreign and domestic carrier. Ronald Allen, Robert Crandall and Stephen Wolf—chairmen and CEOs of their companies—spoke out jointly against the partial acquisition and investment proposed by British Airways in USAir. The British backed away from that deal when it was seriously questioned, but another deal was attempted and completed later. Who will command United States air carriers in time of war when they are jointly owned and regulated by two nations and two sets of giant corporations that may disagree on what to do? Who will coerce the giant American corporation with multinational business into obeying the will of the majority of the United States nation when the multinational corporation claims home base elsewhere in the world? What is the meaning of home base if a corporation is chartered in the State of Delaware when international relations are critical? Will the State of Delaware, the home charter state of many major corporations, need to assert itself in international affairs when its corporations are involved? Will this state action conflict with the federal constitution that gives the United States government primary treaty authority in international relations? Or do we now need federal chartering of multinational corporations because domestic and foreign multinational corporations seriously impinge upon national sovereignty and freedom in many diverse and undesirable ways? These questions we will tackle shortly.

National Sovereignty

The key to understanding national freedom is observing how a nation is discussing its freedom at any particular time. Three external historical threats to the United States illustrate this point quite well. The first threat of an external nature caused repression at home when the Alien and Sedition Acts were passed by Congress in 1798. Relations with France were poor. Liberty of the press and speech were threatened as well as the idea of loyal opposition. Seven years after the Bill of Rights passed, the same founding fathers engaged in a "quasi-war" with France, and the Federalists pushed and passed four national laws of suppression affecting naturalization, deportation and sedition, all directed towards aliens. There was an uproar over this action. The second threat came in the 1930s when, according to Kammen, large numbers of Americans felt European political developments made them realize their heritage of liberty was taken for granted. "For the first time in many, many years, liberty tended to be discussed in terms of external threats rather than in terms of internal structures of governmental authority and domestic disorder and disability."[27]

The external threat of the 1930s never ended. By the 1950s, there were subversive activities laws and the Internal Security Act of 1950, the Communist Control Act of 1954 plus congressional investigations that constrained civil liberties. Kammen said, "For many Americans, security may very well have become a higher priority than either liberty or justice."[28] This observation by Kammen illustrates precisely how other values such as justice, security or fear of foreign subversion or attack will tend to dominate liberty. The intention is clear if the example is well understood. The third example is the immediate relocation of Americans of Japanese ancestry after the Japanese attack on Pearl Harbor on December 7, 1941. In this case, security of American West Coast borders during war justified, in the minds of everyone in power, forcing 120,000 persons—many Japanese American citizens from the West Coast—to relocate into barbed wired camps in the deserts to the east and elsewhere. Burns said, "No protesting voice of consequence was raised as Americans watched their friends and neighbors lose their most precious possession, liberty. Few wondered why Japanese were penned up but not Germans or Italians."[29] Recently reparations were finally paid to the relocated persons but much was lost by these people that will never be regained with money.

National and Corporate Giant Sovereignties

The groundwork is now laid to examine national freedom as it affects the operations of the multinational and the Fortune 500 corporations in

America. The entire history of the American experience with business is basically positive, but this does not mean that both the past and present of the darker side of business should be ignored. That history has much to teach America. This darker side of 100 years of American business directly challenges the idea that free enterprise as a business philosophy was ever meant to be free from government intervention in the market. Freedom in a market often depends upon the goodwill of other competitors and the watchful eyes of the government to assure that freedom to compete will continue, especially for smaller businesses. A brief excursion through the last 100 years of American business will focus on this negative side that threatens freedom of all businesses and of society itself, especially national freedom.

Serving Two Masters

No man can serve two masters; for either he will hate the one, and love the other; or else he will hold to the one and despise the other. Ye cannot serve God and mammon. Matthew 6:24

Mammonism is the greedy pursuit of riches. Plutocracy is the rule or power of the wealth or of the wealthy. A government or a state may have plutocratic classes ruling it. The admission price to the ruling class is wealth. Mammonism propels admission. What is most important to note is that the prevailing attitude in the business community is that this economic state of affairs is considered to be a desirable state of affairs in a free enterprise business economy. The unwritten norm is that there is no limit to upper officer CEO salary and pay disparity. Graef S. Crystal in *In Search of Excess: The Overcompensation of American Executives* (1991) wants, at a minimum, the world to be aware of at least one fact about fairness between workers and chief executive officers (CEO): "In the last twenty years the pay of American workers has gone nowhere, while American CEOs have increased their own pay more than 400 percent." Crystal continued,

You should keep in mind that in 1989, the year when the average major CEO in the United States was earning $2.8 million [a year], the average worker in the private, nonagricultural sector was earning $355.20 per week, or $17,430 per year. Hence, the average major company CEO was earning about 160 times the pay of the average United States worker.[30]

In Derek Bok's *The Cost of Talent: How Executives and Professionals Are Paid and How It Affects America* the same theme is pursued in a broader context in 1993. Liberty of CEO salary levels is not limited by equality. In fact, the president of the United States has a 1991 salary of $200,000. The relevance of the data merely serves to emphasize a basic belief of absence of limit to CEO salary and bonus income in the giant corporation—a true definition of selective economic freedom in the modern American corporation and its relationship to the state and society. This analysis does not begin to examine the fringe benefits, the extreme cases of pay ($275 million for one person from 1973 through 1989 or $16 million a year for the period) or other aspects such as the relationship of poor corporate performance and rising CEO pay. The picture of greed is clear. Mammonism has won the soul of many CEOs. The downsizing turmoil in giant corporations in 1990-1994 is no surprise in view of this outlandish egoism of corporate CEOs and the pay levels demanded and accepted by them.

If greed alone were the only characteristic of American business, it would not even be worth commenting upon in this book devoted to freedom and its definition. Curiously, though, "money talks and big money talks loud," and it should alert us to the underlying ethical norm and the moral postulate—that freedom has no limit in paying top executives of giant corporations in modern America. It is a normless activity where the wishes of other employees for higher salaries are limited, where the dividends for shareholders are limited and where the value of the corporation is apparently meaningless. Egocentric decision making is clearly visible. But the greed or mammon factors are merely an indicator of the basic attitude towards money at the top in American business. No public relations cover-up can conceal this fact. Another indicator is the attitude towards America during war that borders on treason. This is treachery—a direct threat to national freedom.

The attitude of a business person during World War II was captured by Edwin H. Sutherland in his *White Collar Crime* book published first by Dryden Press in 1949. In the uncut, uncensored version published in 1983 by Yale University Press, the names of offending companies, the names of offending officers of corporations and other details eventually made it to print with commentary. The chapter on business war crimes examined how American businesses violated special war regulations, evaded taxes, restrained trade of war materials, maintained competitive positions, violated embargoes and neutrality acts, and committed treason in the sense of revealing military secrets to other nations. The DuPont businesses were involved as were other major businesses. "Patriotism is a very beautiful thing, but it must not be permitted to interfere with business," said Eugene Grace, then president of Bethlehem Steel.[31] Sutherland quoted Lamont DuPont:

The way to view this issue is this: Are there common denominators for winning the war and peace? If there are, then we shall deal with both in 1943. What are they? We will win the war (a) by reducing taxes on corporations and high income brackets, and increasing taxes on low incomes; (b) by removing the unions from any power to tell industry how to produce, how to deal with employees, or anything else; (c) by destroying any and all government agencies that stand in the way of free enterprise.[32]

Dupont's definition for free enterprise in the middle of World War II is egocentric mammonism—endless enrichment at the expense of others. It is the same attitude President Abraham Lincoln mentioned earlier, saying some saw liberty in taking the bread other men made. Sutherland concluded: "Since these corporations lacked the consideration for the general social welfare in an emergency that endangered all civilization, they will be even more incapable of participating in national policies in ordinary years."[33] Think of this in the light of Political Action Committees of the Fortune 500 in federal elections and think, too, that these are many of the same corporate empires that exist today with different men at the helm. Many of them see no limit to their pay. Compare what Camus and Judge Hand said for a different view of liberty during World War II. Whose view of liberty is superior?

To update this 1940s perspective of Sutherland, it is easy to turn to *Putting People First: How We Can All Change America* (1992) by Governor Bill Clinton and Senator Al Gore. The chapter on corporate responsibility makes plain the political strategy of the Clinton Administration with regard to its vision of free enterprise. "Our national economic strategy will reward the people who work hard and play by the rules—the people who create new jobs, start new businesses, and invest in our people and our plants here at home." [34] Selling companies and their workers "down the river"—"shut down plants here and ship our jobs overseas"—"rewarding excess CEO pay," these are themes to link pay and performance in the same sense Graef Crystal argued, to require investment in America, to get tough on polluters and to change workers' conditions such as for family leave, improved labor-management cooperation, continuing education and training and health care. President Clinton's and Vice President Gore's definition of national freedom makes multinational corporations take notice of the future reality conveyed somewhat unequivocally. It makes clear where national loyalties would fit into a hierarchy of importance in the marketplace compared with business loyalties and which set of loyalties should come first. It is the assertion of democratic majority political dominance over a plutocratic order in business in the name of national freedom, popular sovereignty, legal sovereignty and *autonomia* in the classic Greek sense of the word. In 1993, federal law impacted on CEO pay in the new tax act by limiting deductibility of salaries over $1,000,000 a year in some circumstances with shareholder involvement.

The historians would certainly ask us to remember the roots described in *The Robber Barons*, first published in 1934 with a 1962 edition by the author, Matthew Josephson. He surveyed the post Civil War flowering of the industrial revolution in America. The names of the characters are well known: Jay Cooke, Jay Gould, Andrew Carnegie, Pierpont Morgan, John D. Rockefeller, the Vanderbilts and a host of lesser figures. The excesses of this group, the booms and busts are well documented. Two significant threads of intellectual work—the difficult and corrupt historical nature of the American businesses and corporations and their definition of free enterprise, and the thread of white collar crime activities both grew out of this early history of industrialization. "Operation Ill Wind"—a contemporary scandal of Defense Department businesses—and the savings and loan scandals are simply normal business crime. Further documentation of the darker side of American business is found in Ralph Nader, Mark Green and Joel Seligman, *Taming The Giant Corporation* (1976); in Marshall B. Clinard and Peter C. Yeager's *Corporate Crime* (1980); and in Marshall B. Clinard, *Corporate Corruption, The Abuse of Power* (1990)—the last book being dedicated "to those corporations that do not abuse their power." No one who is knowledgeable argues that all Fortune 500 corporations are abusers of their commercial free enterprise. These authors and several more provide both the striking evidence and detail to reveal the darker continuous side of American corporate life that is faithfully and fully explained in vivid detail every day in the *Wall Street Journal*. The definition of free enterprise that emerges from this analysis is that widespread persistent corruption touches on many of the Fortune 500 corporations and their executives. The definition of business freedom and free enterprise is significantly tarnished in this perspective. It suggests that a "buyer beware" philosophy is sensible and that public agencies, some thirty federal agencies (FTC, SEC, FDA, etc.) and hundreds of the state agencies (e.g., weights and measures), are the only sensible antidote that is appropriate to the definitions of free enterprise that heartlessly has included and today includes crime, fraud, waste, abuse and corruption. The savings and loan industry scandal is an example well known in general by the American public, and its tax bills in the foreseeable future will be making justice for harmed depositors. These definitions of free enterprise exclude national well-being and public interest and are limited by justice.

This exposition of national freedom has one twist to it that is found in books as different as Alice M. Rivlin's *Reviving The American Dream* (1992); Donald L. Bartlett and James B. Steele, *America: What Went Wrong?* (1992); Erik Larson, *The Naked Consumer* (1992) and William Greider, *Who Will Tell The People?* (1992). In these works, the authors examine different facets of the American economy, all indicating general malaise: Rivlin analyzes the need to rethink federalism; Larson analyzes the intrusion of market researchers into private lives; and Bartlett and Steele offer a global examination of the American business and economy. Bartlett and Steele noted (1) a middle class hurting economically; (2) an export of American factories and jobs; (3) a shift in taxes to the middle class from the upper income earners; (4) massive bankruptcies; (5) global impacts beyond the American law; (6) deregulation wrecking businesses such as steel and airlines; (7) the health insurance crisis; (8) disappearing of pension funds and the connection to Congress and the president of all of this chaos. The conclusions of Bartlett and Steele are that the rules were changed, no referee existed and no one was looking after the interests of the middle class. Each of these analyses points to serious trouble in defining national freedom in a global economy—none better than William Greider and his analysis. This is another limitless freedom area, just like unlimited CEO salaries. One can hear an echo of Donohue's "anything goes" theme.

The decayed condition of American democracy exists as a reality, just as the Soviet Union disintegrated. This is irony of the highest order for the entire world to observe. Communism fails, democracy decays—nothing succeeds could be the lesson learned. But Greider made it plain:

Why should Americans, for instance, provide research and development tax subsidies for corporations that intend to export their new production and to violate common standards of decency by exploiting the weak? Why should American military forces be deployed to protect companies that do not reciprocate the national loyalty? [35]

This is the sense of betrayal that is emerging in national freedom defined as multinational giant corporation sovereignty.

Greider sees a new global feudalism rising in which American and other giant multinational corporations are rivals for power across the globe, warring like knights in armor for markets and oblivious to local interests and little people. The stateless multinationals in the closet dictator role will be making secret and private alliances and encouraging other alliances that nations may find extremely disloyal and distressing. The corporate strategy will be playing off weak states or nations against one another to compete for plant site selection and for tax concessions to locate factories. Or threats to close plants and move overseas may be made. America's fifty states are also well aware of this political gambit of foreign and domestic businesses. The middle class is reduced in all nations to serfs of the European Middle Ages style and vintage. "If national laws are rendered impotent, then so are a nation's citizens," said Greider.[36] No one has seen the threatened vision of the future of national freedom better than William Greider. His Middle

Ages in Europe analogy is exactly on point. And, new forms of slavery associated with serfs and their lords may not be too far off into the future. Recall that Harold Berman described the European system of slavery in the Middle Ages as did Orlando Patterson in Chapter 5 of his book. These two descriptions in 1983 and 1991 offer a vivid feeling for the future nature of the freedom of the nation under attack by multinational corporations from across the globe.

It has an odd ring—a medieval future. This is certainly not a far-fetched view of national freedom being lost, because the essence of sovereignty is taken from a nation by simply spanning its boundaries. Capital is destructively mobile. Think of the Catholic Church as a nation-spanning organization with its own agendas, notably on abortion. Multiply the Catholic Church by 1000 or more multinational corporations around the globe. Greider thinks the decay of democracy is not yet complete, but if anything needs attention, it is the attention to protect national freedom. It is the health of American democracy and national sovereignty that must be put first in defining the meaning of free enterprise and manufacturing in tomorrow's economy. Susan and Martin Tolchin offer an excellent thesis about the challenge to American national freedom in *Selling Our Security: The Erosion of America's Assets* (1992). The Tolchins said about national sovereignty, "Dealing with that fact of life represents one of the biggest challenges of our times." [37] The fact of life to which they refer is the manipulation of nations by multinational giants threatening national sovereignty by playing off one nation against another.

William Greider and Susan and Martin Tolchin among others are touching the same reality. It is national freedom and its imperilment by irresponsible visions of national freedom without any significant concern for the public interest of a majority of citizens of a nation. By contrast, James Madison supported popular sovereignty of all Americans in 1787. The middle-class majority today senses this deep trouble—treacherous trouble in its future in this facet of national freedom. The fight over the NAFTA Agreement in 1993 merely highlights the nature of this fight. [38]

To illustrate just how serious the issue of national and popular sovereignty has become, one only has to see the advanced praise of Richard Nixon, George Shultz and Henry Kissinger on the jacket of Walter B. Wriston's book *The Twilight of Sovereignty* (1992). The importance of this book in its challenge to national freedom is that the former chairman of Citicorp is the author, Walter Wriston. Citicorp is an American corporation with a global reach. Its capital is mobile; its home base could be anywhere on earth. As one involved in global markets using modern information technology, Wriston knows that knowledge is a key to future success, and knowledge lies in information networks of computers and satellites. Offshore money launderers know this as well. Wriston knows that technology respects the boundaries of no nation. And knowledge is power. Wriston argued that borders of nations are not boundaries, that global market conversations cannot be stopped or even be well monitored at borders, and that currency may be denationalized. "The old political boundaries of nation-states," Wriston writes, "are being made obsolete by an alliance of commerce and technology." [39] This reinforces the views of William Greider. How true that statement is rapidly becoming. If boundaries are obsolete, what about the laws of nations? Are these obsolete as well, as Greider suggested? Or is it true as Thomas Jefferson wrote in a letter to Horatio G. Spafford on March 17, 1814: "Merchants have no country. The mere spot they stand on does not constitute so strong an attachment as that from which they draw their gains."

Wriston noted that the exact country of origin of a product may not be known; labels on integrated electronic circuits are stamped to say, "The exact country of origin is unknown." [40] We have heard this before in white-collar crime. This is very strange that business can purposely *not* keep track of sources of supply from vendors, but it seems falsely contrived as well to serve other real business needs to avoid regulation or taxation by a nation. We all know that commercial fraud starts with such purposefully designed confusion. Confusion of supply sources can be deliberately set up by a business, if desired. Three different sets of accounting books can be kept by a computer, if desired. This fits into another myth of Wriston and others—that the greatest danger in the world is protectionism. Protectionism of one's job is outmoded thinking I would surmise. For a laid-off American worker, this is the kind of thinking about national freedom that giant corporations are trying to take over as their own form and definition of corporate global sovereignty.

In an even odder way, Wriston acknowledged that information technologies affect governments, but there seems to be no twilight in the future of the Fortune 500 corporations and their trade secrets and business privacy caused by the same technology except perhaps for the Graef Crystal exposés of CEOs compensation. Wriston stated, "In the new world, *we may not see corporate democracies,* but we will see the skills of the manager outstripped by the demand for leadership." [41] One could wonder why *both* national boundaries of states and multinational corporate boundaries would not be stripped away simultaneously by such all powerful, modern, information technologies. Will the nation-state wither away in importance while the Fortune 500 and multinational corporations thrive in their information-based, high-tech global alliances? How can the information revolution produce such disparate results? Wriston sounded a bit like Karl Marx and his mistaken prediction of the withering away of the state. And he seems to be about as correct as Marx. As if to assuage us, Wriston wrote:

The information technology, which carries the news of freedom, is rapidly creating a situation that might be described as the twilight of sovereignty, since the absolute power of the state to act alone both internally against its own citizens and externally against other nations' affairs is rapidly being attenuated. *This does not mean that the nation-state will disappear*; indeed, we will see more countries formed.[42]

The nation-state of the future, even the United States, is viewed ultimately as a weakling gorilla in the face of a giant corporation and its invasive modern technology. This seems to be more gee-whiz logic of the information age.

Popular sovereignty raises more questions than Wriston answers. Who makes the laws and enforces them? Who fights the wars? Who taxes the people? Who fights for national freedom? Who dies? Apparently Wriston's view is that several thousand giant corporations across the globe (allowing weak nation-states to exist) are either to become harmonious cartels (never steal trade secrets) or to become beneficent corporate giants thinking always of the welfare of the other little guy and his liberty—his national liberty? It sounds to me to be an unreal future given the tendencies of giant corporations to gobble up competitors at the slightest provocation. America has not experienced three major merger waves in 100 years of business life because competition is so much desired by the Fortune 500. Can you imagine the fate of governments if left to sovereign fortunes of the Fortune 500 and other global multinational giants? Their state sovereignty would have been stripped long ago. We still live with that terrible threat today.[43]

PART II. FREEDOM WITHIN A STATE OR NATION: CIVIC LIBERTY

The principal distinguishing characteristics of freedom within a state or nation are these:

1. By the logic of the other two parts of freedom, this aspect of liberty is *not* national freedom just explained with examples, and it is *not* inner liberty, yet to be defined fully in this chapter with examples.
2. Freedom within the state is found in the structure and procedures of a state. Written constitutions, federalism and separation of powers are examples of structural features designed to protect liberty of citizens. The right to vote and right to participate in civil government by holding office are more of the same.
3. When most of the constitutional structure has been established for 200 years, as it has been in America, many ignore or lose sight completely of the organizational design of the nation and states that

relates to freedom of citizens. We follow the past in an unthinking way.

4. The limits of governmental power over citizens are foremost in the minds of those who think about freedom within a state or nation. This concern is similar to the third aspect of freedom—inner liberty with the human rights and Bill of Rights logic permeating that area. Thomas Jefferson's admonition to give eternal vigilance to freedom and the struggle to keep it supports and energizes concern here.

Ancient Logic and Origins

Freedom is acknowledged by a number of scholars of ancient Greece to be a central value in that early society. Slavery of human beings was widespread, and this enhanced the understanding of what it meant to be free. The ancient Greeks acknowledged the important necessity of freedom under law as a contribution to desirable order. The society in Greece from about 600 B.C. to about 400 B.C.— from Solon to Cleisthenes to Pericles— moved from popular sovereignty to sovereignty of law.[44] The rule of law and equal distribution of rights (*isonomia*) were wedded to these systems. Democracy became a part of the structure. Juries were used extensively.

Perhaps Victor Ehrenberg articulated the link of two parts of freedom (between freedom within a state and the third aspect inner liberty) by saying, "It is the greatness of the Periclean ideal that freedom under the law also permits, indeed seems to guarantee, the free development of personality."[45] Ehrenberg believed the unconditional unity of liberty and obedience to law is illustrated by Socrates'death— suffering an injustice but accepting the verdict of the people's tribunal and convinced that no individual has the right to weaken the authority of law.

Another important observation of Ehrenberg is this:

Freedom and democracy were closely related concepts, but not identical; they both displayed many and various shades of meaning. The vital point is that in democracy the idea of equality went side-by-side with the idea of freedom, and often enough took its place; what mattered was collective freedom as the will of the majority.[46]

The ancient Greeks offered the world an extraordinary array of rich ideas to consider in governing—especially self-governing. The influence on Roman thinking, the long disappearance of the Greek thought and its reemergence again much later in Western Civilization is some evidence of the attractive vitality of these ideas.

A Reawakening Influence in Europe: 1600-1780

Freedom within a state or nation was on the agenda of English and French philosophers. John Locke (1632-1704) in his *Second Treatise of Government* (1691) and Montesquieu (1689-1755) in his *The Spirit of the Laws* (1748) provided intellectual grounding for Jean Jacques Rousseau (1712-1778) in his *Social Contract* (1762). The significance for America of this intellectual heritage Kammen made plain:

Those who framed the Constitution drew most heavily for guidance upon the American experience with political realities during the preceding quarter of a century. In so far as they heeded intellectual influences, especially external ones, a single source is cited more than all others combined: Montesquieu's *Spirit of the Laws* (1748).[47]

Kammen's further insight with Montesquieu is critical for the distinctions among aspects of freedom attempted in this book:

It should be acknowledged directly that that influential work [*The Spirit of the Laws*] enhanced the meaning of liberty by *clarifying* the distinction between freedoms embodied in a constitution as a system of government (liberty inherent in the procedures of a state) and the freedoms to which private persons were entitled by national right and custom (emphasis supplied).[48]

This clarifying distinction justified marking a special place for freedom within a state as a system of governance. From the very beginning of this book, I have stressed the necessity of clarity in defining liberty if any advances are to be made in thinking about it. Here is an exceptionally valuable observation by Kammen that assists us greatly in defining freedom within a state and distinguishing it from freedom from a state. Kammen is independent and is consistent with Victor Ehrenberg's independent insight into ancient Greek distinctions of a similar character. Inner liberty in the sense that John Stuart Mill defined it in 1859 in *On Liberty* is distinguishable from freedom within a state, because it aims not to use the state powers, but aims to keep the government out of certain areas of life.

Early American Logic and Origins

Kammen observed, "It seems reasonable to assert that the colonists gradually 'discovered' liberty during the seventeenth century, and then became obsessed by it during the course of the eighteenth." [49] The theme of liberty confined by a greater need for authority was found by Michael

Kammen in John Winthrop's speech on liberty, July 3, 1645, to the General Court of the Massachusetts Bay Colony. The same theme appeared in England in John Locke's *Second Treatise of Government* (1691), in David Hume's essay "Of the Origin of Government" and in William Blackstone's *Commentaries*. The theme of property and its protection as a constraint on liberty is found in the literature. What emerged from this early American concern for liberty and the need to create a new nation meant eventually that among many others Alexander Hamilton (1757-1804), Thomas Jefferson (1743-1826) and James Madison (1751-1836) were thrust into central roles—using both the American and European experience and European and American sources to concoct such a new nation, create its government and design the relationships between states and a central government. The *Federalist* was a source of logic to protect liberty. Furthermore, Jefferson liked the idea of separation of powers into legislative, judiciary and executive. Madison wrote in 1788 that preservation of liberty requires separation of powers. Hamilton agreed on separation of powers citing Montesquieu, and he argued that liberty and property would need to be accommodated. The design of the federal constitution and its adoption in 1787, and the design of the Bill of Rights and its adoption in 1791 are the foundation for federalism as we know it today and for separation of powers into three major branches. Liberty is the value to be protected—democracy to be advanced by such elaborate designs.

The following elements of liberty are specific examples of what freedom within a nation or state means or has grown to mean in America over the last 200 years of national development.

1. The Right to Vote. Expanding the voting list to nonproperty owners, blacks, women and younger persons is the key to a growing electorate. *Baker v. Carr* 369 U.S. 186 (1962) is the one-person, one-vote historical decision logic that has strengthened this aspect of liberty and required periodic reapportionment nationwide to improve representativeness of elected bodies. Whether citizens will vote is a separate question.

2. The Right to Hold Office. The number of such offices, the quality of officials, the breadth of representative government in a federal government, fifty state governments, 3,000 counties and over 10,000 cities and thousands more of special districts, shows a growth and expansion in a democracy of, by and for the people. Transferring power from generation to generation has been worked out successfully in all these transitions.

3. The Right to Tax Incomes and Estates. This egalitarian constitutional order is significant in shaping the liberty of accumulating wealth and passing it on. It is coupled with an antimonopoly attitude in American society and law. Equality clearly limited and shaped the liberty to earn, save and do business—that is the American Dream.

4. The Right to Speak Politically. This freedom is not restrained in any unreasonable way in 1993. There is concern over access to expensive mass media, but no one thinks there is not sufficient liberty of speech and press in matters of a political nature. With the dying of the old Cold War and secrecy needs, there is an area opening up. The *Selling of Our Security* (1992) by the Tolchins is an important factor here to constrain industrial and commercial secrets and intellectual property. As for censorship, Nat Hentoff in *Free Speech for Me, But Not for Thee* (1992) sheds light on strange new problems of free speech.

5. The Right to Be Valued As a Person. The civil rights acts eventually have produced some of the respect and equal opportunity desired by the black community. School integration decisions and equal opportunity laws underscored the rising value of the equality. The expansion of equal rights to sexual harassment laws, disabled person laws, and concerns over health care and pension funds and deep concern over housing show more clearly the nature of freedom in a socially conscious society. Some call this the "welfare society," but that seems to connote weakness and gifts to poor by the rich—not at all relevant to the value of each person in America.

Two topics are candidates to review for the application of the idea of transformed freedom within a state. The first topic is the problem of cultural diversity in American society and its relationship to freedom within a state. The second topic is the problem and need of rebalancing federal-state relationships in their relationship to freedom within a state.

American Dream of Freedom and the Melting Pot

The normal and dominant way for a new citizen is to assimilate, to melt into the society. The question of assimilation into the general culture of America is the same thing as saying that when people dream of coming to America, say from Cuba, Haiti, Canada, Mexico or any number of places they dream of assimilating into the larger society by speaking the same language, paying the same taxes, eating the same food, wearing the same clothes, sending children to American public schools, and attending the church of their choice. Assimilating is the goal of the melting pot so that a new American citizenship is achieved by naturalization before an American federal judge and by taking an oath to support and defend the Constitution that gains citizenship status. Freedom within the state is extremely valuable to the assimilated—the right to vote, for example. The idea of freedom of the nation for the new citizen is important to protect that citizen in and from the rest of the world. Freedom from the nation is significant because it guarantees the right to worship whatever way one wishes. People every day risk their lives to reach the American Dream of Freedom.

The norm of complete assimilation has never been totally effective or desired by every immigrant. Some immigrants return to their home nation. Others retain as much of the manners, habits, language and ideas of the former nation as possible—at least through the first generation. But the children born in America usually assimilate unless they are in some unique subculture—say the Amish culture in Ohio and Pennsylvania. The subcults of America are not just subcultures; some are nations with treaties in their own right within the United States. American constitutional freedom is the general pattern with exceptions: for Amish, for Indian tribes and others. There are unifying themes; there are disunifying themes. Some Swedes and Germans in the midwestern United States retained much of their culture, at least some attempted to create enclaves of difference. Some Chinese in San Francisco or ex-Cubans in Miami reflect nonassimilation.

Since 1954, the years of growth in racial rectification in America, some blacks (a minority) argued for a separate nation in the United States. These separatists were of the same mind as the Quebec French separatists. All are nonassimilation types—"nonmelting potists"—if I may be permitted to create a clear nonassimilation attribute and attitude. The American Dream of Freedom is dealt a serious blow by this approach to citizenship for new immigrants. But, for American Indians, nonassimilation has been their goal of separation—thus reservations and separate Indian nations. For blacks who have been here since the early 1600s—who are true natives who did not even begin to have a right to share in the American Dream of Freedom until 1865, and who spent the years of reconstruction being put down, and who spent a further period until the 1960s wondering about the American Dream of Freedom—all of the talk about the American Dream of Freedom must have seemed hollow and rather false to them. One can understand why blacks in less than one recent generation in America are finally "feeling their oats" as citizens. They are experiencing more freedom within the nation.

It is in this context that one should appreciate Lawrence Fuchs in *The American Kaleidoscope: Race, Ethnicity, and Civic Culture* (1990) and Arthur M. Schlesinger, Jr. in *The Disuniting of America, Reflections on a Multicultural Society* (1992). Both authors argue for an explanation of the American Dream of Freedom based upon the idea of strength in diversity, one out of many, *e pluribus unum*. Diversity as a source of national identity and source of national unity is a logical way that a polyglot society of people from across the globe can come together. In religion this has been most effective-- all religions are equal. In cultures—all cultures have good elements in them; the same for races and ethnics. For Baltimore—its cultural diversity is a source of community pride in annual celebrations across the city—not a source of divisiveness or disunity. Annual cultural fairs on the mall in Washington, D.C. reflect this parallel attitude of diversity and unity defining the American Dream.

The United States is developing a common culture of its own that is based upon many cultures. To use a rather meaningless term, America is "multicultural." This is a truism about American freedom within the state to assert cultural and religious differences since the beginning of colonies. States such as Maryland were settled by people being persecuted for religious beliefs in England. The growth from 1600 to 1800 and the 1787 emergence of the United States Constitution and the Bill of Rights in 1791 show the overlay of national order, the constitutional order of unity, cultural unity in a Bill of Rights. Schlesinger said it best:

Our democratic principles contemplate an open society founded on tolerance of differences and on mutual respect. In practice, America has been more open to some than to others. But it is more open to all today than it was yesterday and is likely to be even more open tomorrow than today. The steady movement of American life has been from exclusion to inclusion.[50]

The phrase, "liberty and justice for all," in the pledge of allegiance is aligned with inclusion.

Like the agnostic, humanist or atheist in religion, the American Dream of Freedom also makes room for all Americans who want no peculiar cultural ties beyond being American first, last and only. There are many Americans who want nothing to do with organized religion or with a separate non-American culture whether it is Spanish, Greek, Italian, Irish or identified by a skin color or religion. The American Dream of Freedom also includes those who aspire to all of the cultural nuances that they can dream up, and then wear, eat, sing, talk or think to make themselves believe they are different. Freedom within the state in the American Dream of Freedom means the absence of an orthodox culture or religion, but it does not mean absence of an overriding American culture highlighted by the right to vote in a constitutional democracy and the Bill of Rights, a minimal level of limiting government in America. Freedom within a state means, at least, that much. We have agreed to disagree in a civil manner about many things to make democracy work in a civilized manner.

The American Dream of Freedom is centered on freedom within a state of certain characteristics, not upon a cultural orthodoxy, but upon a heterodoxy of cultural diversity. This fits in well with the third part of freedom—freedom from a state which itself generates further extraordinary diversity in ideas and cultures. The clear result is that the American melting pot works well with some immigrants, less well with some displaced and rightfully disgruntled American Indians, and less well with alienated subgroups within the culture such as some Hispanic and black groups in parts of America. You can bet that most of these people are poor economically as well. However, most Americans of any color are not alienated and not culturally lost in modern America. Instead they are Americans first and foremost with a powerful general American culture to support them. This is true for the Finnish or Jewish or Puerto Rican or Afro-Americans.

Freedom Within a State or Nation Having Federalism and Separation of Powers for Constitutional Order

The next application of the idea of freedom within a state or nation is so basic we ignore it at times. It is so important that our *inattention* to it may be perilous to America. The idea of federalism seems so simple because we in America live with it every day. It is like saying "the sun rises." We have the fifty states and the United States government. The separation of powers into legislative, executive and judicial is the same contemptuously familiar "the moon rises." So what else is new? That these designs of government were thought up, enacted into a wide range of fifty-one constitutions in America and have lasted for a long period of time makes them less than thrilling to discuss. All of that is true. A useful way to see the diffusion of power by deliberate choice and its effect on freedom within the state is to consider the extreme alternative of a tyranny, one-man rule, a despotism (benevolent or harsh) or a totalitarian order where the state is all-encompassing in life. One way to see freedom within a state is to imagine the Nazis or Saddam Hussein in charge of the United States. No federalism, only unity of the nation and states and no separation of powers into three branches would exist. No constitutional order, no labor unions, no churches, no business groups, no civic groups, no political parties, no private groups—just one-man and a small clique rule. It sounds like Cuba, Romania and Iraq. These are obviously extremes in the patterns of governance that are much richer than indicated in reality.

Diffused and segmented powers of government are a basic part of the American Dream of Freedom within a state. "Divide and conquer" is an ancient adage seen by Montesquieu, by the English (his model) and by the founding fathers of the American government in considering federal order and separation of powers in the design of the federal constitution and most state constitutions.[51] One divides and separates government power and places checks and balances on each branch *So That No One Can Create a Tyranny!* This fact is so obvious it is often forgotten or overlooked. Gridlock, the famous term in the 1992 federal elections, is nothing more than constitutional design thwarting someone's political ambitions.

Gridlock is a part, a normal part, of constitutional design. It is desirable because it produces political change, and it eventually forces compromise and cooperation.

The doctrine of the separation of powers has a long English history—just as the hundreds of years of development lie behind the English monarchy, the same for the Parliament, and the same for the judiciary—the latter being secured independently by 1701. By contrast, Andrei Vyshinsky, a leading Soviet legal authority did not think separation of powers fit in the "new order" of communism. And, on January 30, 1934, when Nazi power was becoming absolute in Germany, according to Arthur T. Vanderbilt, this meant an end to any idea of separation of powers there. The legislative and judicial functions were totally usurped by an executive tyranny in Germany. Nothing stood in the way to limit the power of Hitler.

The extraordinarily opposite view of freedom within a state is embodied in the American constitutional order. The most vivid statement about separation of powers comes from Arthur T. Vanderbilt, former Chief Justice of the Supreme Court of New Jersey. Vanderbilt wrote: "The doctrine [of separation of powers] must be universal in its application if stability and liberty are to be sought and obtained." [52] If stability and liberty are to be sought or obtained, these separated powers are the secret "genius factors" behind the long-term stability of England and the United States. Political stability is valuable if liberty is respected. These ideas of separation of powers are just as significant for the liberty in both nations as their bills of rights. Vanderbilt's dream of universality of separation of powers is still a dream, but it is obvious that the idea offers a desirable state of affairs wherever it is taken seriously. The federal distribution of power and the separation of powers are the most significant part of the "genius of the American government" in its structural bias towards liberty and stability as simultaneously valuable goals.   Other nations benefit in the same way—Canada, Australia.

Federalism has "no right answers" according to Alice M. Rivlin in *Reviving The American Dream: The Economy, The States and The Federal Government* (1992). But she makes a case for rethinking federalism: which level of government should do what and where should the revenues come from. Rivlin argues that the impact of global interdependence, the need to carry out reform at the local level first (bottom up), the general need for more tax revenues in all government in general are reasons to rethink federal ordering. However, she does not include the most important reason to reconsider federalism, that is, to protect liberty of citizens more carefully. The freedom within a state or nation that is so central a part of the American Dream may be threatened by excessive centralized power. This omission is puzzling. The case she makes does make sense without even considering what happens to freedom within the state. But it seems much less significant in the long run.

The history of what has happened to federalism in America in exquisite detail is found in the United States Advisory Commission on Intergovernmental Relations (ACIR), *A Commission Report, Federal Statutory Preemption of State and Local Authority: History, Inventory, and Issues,* September 1992. The report stated, "There has been a dramatic increase in federal statutory preemption of state and local authority during the last twenty years." [53] The report stated that over 50 percent of 439 preemption statutes passed by Congress were passed in the last *two* decades. The report calls this action by Congress "startling." (See the graph of such action in Appendix 2.) The federal government must have power to function, but "too much of a good thing can be bad." Too much federal power can wreck a federal order, too much preemption may threaten liberty. Too much central authority in Washington could weaken democracy everywhere in the United States of America. Too much central authority and taxing power in Washington could jeopardize freedom in the entire nation by warping the distribution of power, skewing it towards Washington, D.C. Extreme federal supremacy in every matter would reduce federalism to a sort of French bureaucratic central unity coming out of Washington, D.C. This would be a revolution without a bullet being fired.[54] It is a silent revolution.

Why would Congress deliberately threaten federalism in the last twenty years? According to the ACIR report there were many reasons. First, national regulatory functions have increased. Second, restraints by the constitution itself have been interpreted to give more expansion of congressional power. Third, Congress must protect human rights once declared to be so by the Supreme Court. Fourth, federal fiscal capability is reduced through deficits. Fifth, new regulatory areas, for example, environment, have opened. Sixth, Washington interest groups and big businesses push for one regulator—"a gorilla" not "fifty monkeys"—fifty state regulators in fifty states. Seventh, global markets in Europe and Asia want a uniform national market in the entire United States of America, not just uniformity in certain states. Eighth, bipartisan support exists for greater federalization of all government. Ninth, popular support exists for some federal preemption—in safety, health and environment. These factors are contributing to increased preemption and they mean greater, not lesser, national control of the entire nation. Obviously, it means weaker states, reduced local sovereignty, greater threat of growing potential for tyranny from a single source—Washington, D.C.—in the nation. Freedom within a nation with disappearing federalism is a potential disaster for Americans and its history of strong and effective decentralization and strong states. The ACIR saw this clearly and warned against it. Many in Congress and the nation are oblivious—unaware. Global marketeers have no interest in fifty states and have little interest in 178 nations; corporate sovereignty is the only interest they share.

Shadow Governments and Freedom

Who are the terra incognita of government? There are some 35,000 public authorities at federal, state, and local levels—that is, public or government corporations. The Resolution Trust Corporation (RTC) was and is used to resolve the savings and loan scandal, or the New York Port Authority or California Water Authority act in their domains. This invisible government raises billions of tax dollars alongside the visible government, at all levels. The invisible governments are free of control by the public, are free of public surveillance, and are loose cannons of the ship of state. These are the findings of Donald Axelrod in *Shadow Government: The Hidden World of Public Authorities and How They Control Over $1 Trillion of Your Money* (1992). The Federal Savings and Loan Corporation (FSLIC) stamp and seal on the doors of all of the savings and loan banks in the past is now gone, but the FSLIC was part of the savings and loan problem, not just a guarantor of depositor loans. Freedom within a state or nation cannot even be mentioned here, because these corporations are quasi-governmental in nature. There is no state to be free within. It is a quasi-public activity. It runs a course parallel to giant corporations and multinational corporations. It is more difficult to assert public interest when the activity is taken from the public agenda. Freedom within the state is threatened by such covert operations. The impact of freedom within the state is unknown but cannot be anything less than potentially tyrannical in nature.

The example of shadow governments is rich with a feeling that governments should *not* be free to create any subunits they wish to create. The same could be said of giant and multinational corporations. This freedom is not responsive to federalism or separation of powers logic, it fails to keep constitutional order as clear as it should be for the citizen taxpayers. It invites irresponsible evasion of bonding and debt limits, and it suggests extraordinary freedom where most of the public may want what Axelrod suggested is higher levels of accountability and greater degrees of openness. Unlike the federal preemption excesses, the shadow governments are not unbalancing federal-state allocation of responsibilities in a clear public way that is too complex to be understood by the ordinary person; but, instead, these shadow governments have irresponsible hidden freedom to tax, an unaccountable freedom, a destructive force of freedom to confuse the public. It is a form of internal subversion of constitutional order. It is not a responsible federalism in many cases examined by Axelrod. It is similar to the irresponsible giant corporation and its challenges to national and state sovereignty. Public corporations and all private corporations, even the Fortune 500 giants, are chips off the block of state and national sovereignty. No one should forget this basic fact of life in politics, but it seems that we have forgotten. The reasons for this state of affairs and the history of getting into this condition are beyond the bounds of this book, but it is one of the more fascinating stories about America.

PART III. FREEDOM FROM A STATE OR NATION: INNER LIBERTY

What is the nature and what are the limits of the state power which can be legitimately exercised by society through government over an individual? Mill's slightly modified question, he said, is seldom stated or hardly ever discussed, but "it is likely soon to make itself recognized as the vital question of the future." [55] From 1859 to 1994, the 135-year-old statement of Mill has indeed become true. This question is critical for those who fear that Americans have too many liberties and too few as well. It dominates much of the agenda in America, but the antidote to this unbalanced agenda can be seen in the two previous parts of this chapter using Victor Ehrenberg's ideas of liberty. That is, national freedom and freedom within a state or nation are important topics as well. I have just tried to clarify that fact. In this part, the application could include an extremely diverse set of topics—abortion, religious toleration, free speech, freedom of association, artistic freedom, and freedom from invasion by technology of our privacy to name just a few topics.

Before announcing a topic for application of the transformed freedom defined here as the freedom from a state, it is helpful to look first at the difficulty Ehrenberg discovered in ancient Greek literature with regard to inner liberty and why he found such difficulty. Searching for an ancient ancestor to modern inner freedom is not a simple task even for the experts. It may be that there is no equivalence between a Greek city-state and a modern nation, but that does not ring true with what I know.

Ancient Greeks and Inner Liberty

There is no doubt of ancient Greek development of national freedom and freedom within a state. There is some doubt about whether ancient Greeks enjoyed some form of the inner liberty of a freedom from a state in the sense developed in the last few centuries in Western Civilization. Ehrenberg considered "personal liberty" or individual freedom to be an apt description of inner liberty and considered individual artistic freedom to be typical of the freedom from the state. But charges of impiety successfully lodged against significant ancient Greeks (Pericles and Socrates) meant freedom of conscience could not be an ancient right. The way I interpret this state of affairs is that there must have been found contrary evidence that causes uncertainty. Ehrenberg said, "I cannot find with them [ancient Greeks] that absolute realization of individual freedom that many have postulated." [56] "Freedom within the state was a general fact, freedom *from* the state was the exception." [57] Yet Ehrenberg did not overlook Pericles: "It is the greatness of the Periclean ideal that freedom under law also permits, indeed seems to guarantee, the free development of personality." [58] Even though Ehrenberg excluded freedom of conscience from ancient Greek culture, he included jests of the gods in Aristophanes and Homer, and freedom of speech with a presupposition of freedom of thought and discussion. Ehrenberg left the question of Greek ancestorship to modern inner liberty in doubt.

Pericles (494 B.C.-429 B.C.), the leading statesman of Athenian democracy in 5th century B.C. is the source of beliefs that there was "considerable space for individualism and privacy, free from public scrutiny." [59] Donald Kagan in *Pericles of Athens and the Birth of Democracy* (1991) compares favorably the famous funeral oration of Pericles to Abraham Lincoln's funeral oration at Gettysburg in 1863. [60] Both addressed a somber question: Why should citizen's lives be risked for a nation? Both orations address the question to the living. From among possible interpretations, I am inclined to accept Kagan's interpretation of the ancient Greek written by the historian Thucydides. It was Thucydides who wrote a history of the entire funeral oration of Pericles that gave the following partial evidence of an inner liberty for Athenians 2,500 years ago:

Not only do we conduct our public life as freemen but we are also free of suspicion of one another as we go about our every-day lives. We are not angry with our neighbor if he does what pleases him, and we don't glare at him which, even if it is harmless, is a painful sight. [61]

The Periclean ideal of freedom contrasts with Sparta's approach, which most scholars of ancient Greek life seem to agree is an opposite model of life where freedom is minimal, especially inner liberty is minimized. The point of this ancient Greek ancestry is just that; it could well be an ancestor in Western Civilization to the modern view of inner liberty spelled out so fully in writing in the Declaration of the Rights of Man and Citizen in France (1789), the Bill of Rights in the United States (1791), and with the Universal Declaration of Human Rights in 1948 by the United Nations and reemphasized in the 1993 Vienna Declaration and Programme of Action. The freedom from the state or nation is central to these historical documents of basic limits on governmental power. In another sophisticated way, mankind in Western Civilization has sought greater and greater freedom from all constraints of states, churches and religions and society. The furthest reaches of this struggle for freedom from the state exist today, and we are witnesses to this in arguments of too few or too many freedoms spelled out previously in Chapters 2 and 3. The true condition of American inner liberty—freedom from the state—is one where Americans are pushing the ragged edges of reality where no one has been before in past societies. Surely this reasoning helps to account for the difficulty of the abortion debate and assisted suicides. Questions of inner liberty from state control are the frontiers of all aspects of freedom.

Monkeying Around and Inner Liberty: Human Development

None other than the famous Judge Learned Hand offered another reason for being concerned about maximizing the liberty of inquiry. "James Harvey Robinson used to say that we rose from the ape because like him we kept 'monkeying around,' always meddling with everything about us." [62] Hand went on to say:

My thesis is that any organization of society which depresses free and spontaneous meddling is on the decline, however showy its immediate gain; I maintain that in such a society, liberty is gone, little as it members may know it; that the NIRVANA of the individual is too high a price for collective paradise. Because, once you get people believing that there is an authoritative well of wisdom to which they can turn for absolutes, you have dried up the springs on which they must in the end draw even for things of this world. As soon as we cease to pry about at random, we shall come to rely upon accredited bodies of authoritative dogma; and as soon as we come to rely upon accredited bodies of authoritative dogma, not only are the days of our liberty over, but we have lost the password that has hitherto opened us to gates of success as well.[63]

Other judges from the United States Supreme Court reflected on the "prying about at random" or "monkeying around."

Justice Robert H. Jackson (1892-1954)
If there is any fixed star in our constitutional constellation, it is that no official, high or petty, can prescribe what shall be orthodox in politics, nationalism, religion, or other matters of opinion or force citizens to confess by word or act their faith therein. *Minersville School District v. Gobitis* 319 U.S. 624 (642) (1940).

Justice Louis D. Brandeis (1856-1941)
They [the makers of the constitution] conferred, as against the government, the right to be let alone—the most comprehensive of rights and the right most valued by civilized men." *Olmstead v. U.S.* 277 U.S. 438 (478) (1928)

The inner liberty of John Stuart Mill, the monkeying around or random prying of Judge Learned Hand, the lack of orthodoxy in politics, nationalism, religion or other matters of opinion of Justice Robert Jackson and the right to be let alone of Justice Louis Brandeis, all of these expressions are different ways of expressing freedom of thought, freedom of speech, freedom of association, free exercise of religion and free press rights. Martin Luther's (1483-1546) protest against the Catholic Church would never have led to a Lutheran Protestant Church; Galileo's (1564-1642) assertion of a solar system against an earth-centered universe would have failed against the Catholic Church, and all of the other unorthodox beliefs would have failed in the past without faith, trust and "monkeying around" with supposed truths. The prevailing paradigm of thought must be exploded by the truth, and freedom of thought and freedom of expression are central to the inevitable destruction of supposed verities. This questioning goes back to man's origins and affects his entire life. Science is part of this large equation of endless prying about—monkeying around. The imaginative life of poets, musicians, artists, writers, philosophers, lawyers and historians depends on freedom to "pry about."

What could possibly trigger an upsurge in desire for freedom from the state? In America it is too obvious, but it is worth mentioning the cultural forces of homogenization and standardization of industry and businesses and of technology on both government and society; the presence and pressure of 250,000,000 people wanting breakfasts, lunches and dinners, houses to live in, clothes to wear, and 190,000,000 cars and other vehicles to drive to work in every day; the massive governments and huge bureaucracies to serve them; the massive corporations and other private institutions to nurture them; the end of wilderness as it used to be known; and the peculiarly invasive, omnipresent modern technology that sees and hears all. The crazed anthill bureaucratic existence is likely to make any normal person search for freedom in many ways—in religion, in 500 TV cable channels, in sex and pornography, in drugs, and in rock and roll music. Drugs, sex and rock and roll are some of the antidotes to anthill existence where, it seems to some, inner liberty is all that is left to express individuality.

What would be the impact of justice and equality on liberty in the 20th century in America? Kammen argued that justice and equality were the great conditioners of liberty or were the channelers of liberty in this century compared more frequently with the last century when order competed with liberty. Social Security payments must be made; there is no choice in equality. The fundamental shift of the American national government in regulatory and welfare reforms in the 1930s and 1940s ended an excessive business depression era. World War II offered more federal regulatory growth and sound welfare reforms. The powerful themes of social justice kept individual liberty somewhat displaced or not a top priority. In 1993, the health reform needs and parental leave proposals are in the same tradition of social welfare and justice; a free-floating freedom in these matters is not desired by the mass of society that wants more certainty of health care.

The same power of justice and equality to channel liberty can be seen in the decision of 1954, *Brown v. Board of Education of Topeka*, 347 U.S. 483, the equal opportunity acts and affirmative action plans, the desegregated schools, the proposed equal rights amendments for women and the Americans with Disabilities Act. Both justice and equality shaped liberty, especially inner liberty.

Kammen correctly identifies the two major influences on liberty in the last seventy-five years—justice and equality.[64] These contingent values have persuaded the majority to move ahead into deeper reforms with lesser regard for the implications for an individual's freedom from the state. The fact is clear that no matter how much special pleading is done to revive personal responsibility as an antidote to excessive and outrageous forms of inner liberty, personal responsibility as a cause remains a weak tool to channel liberty. Social justice and equality as social forces produce a comparable result, and they are much stronger in changing liberty of those who must be changed to achieve a greater good of justice and equality, say in racial affairs.

In many cases, where this leaves inner liberty or freedom from the state in 1994 is at the fringes of a society worrying about (1) whether small religious subgroups can worship with marijuana or snakes; (2) whether small groups on cable TV can watch videos of pornography; (3) whether sexual deviates from dominant heterosexual norms—lesbians and homosexuals—can come "out of the closet" and openly join America and be open in the American Army, Navy, Air Force and Marines; (4) whether nude dancing is a form of speech; and (5) whether free press exists where there is one press per city or per chain of cities. These, on their face, are not the traditional life-and-death issues of human liberty that generate concern over great censorship and excessive governmental regulation of life, although beneath the surface there may lie a hidden underworld of genuine concern that majorities may miss. Edward De Grazia in *Girls Lean Back Everywhere, the Law of Obscenity and the Assault on Genius* (1992) defends the artist at the fringes of society. Here we are getting closer to Mill's inner liberty, but is a Magna Carta for pornography a life and death issue? I think not, but it is an interesting issue of inner liberty quite often at the fringes of tasteless almost universal vulgarity. These issues do not engage the whole energies of the people; they lack motive power.

There was a struggle for freedom from the state; there is a struggle for freedom from the state; and there will always be a struggle to be free of the state. Whether it is abortion, free press, free speech, free exercise of religion, free association, any of the freedoms are under perpetual state pressure at all times in the past, present and future. It would be delusional to think of any hard-won freedom being won forever. History teaches one thing, which Thomas Jefferson said so eloquently: "Eternal vigilance is the price of liberty." The Greeks thought freedom—national freedom—was a perpetual struggle. The same reality exists for the 20th-century liberty; inner liberty requires a perpetual struggle. In 1923 when Justice McReynolds in *Meyer v. Nebraska*, 262 U.S. 390 (1923) referred to Plato and to Sparta's child-raising practices as *not* constitutional in any state under the American constitution, he was saying we have inner liberty to teach the German language or to not teach the German language to children and no state can command otherwise as Nebraska tried to do.[65] Beyond the state and individual struggles for freedom is the teaching of the German language and any other languages as part of inner liberty.

Some Inner Liberty Beyond Legislative Authority

Placing a subject off-limits to legislation is the prerogative of the American people who created and amended the constitution and the people who continue to live by the constitution. The role of the Supreme Court of the United States to declare a subject beyond the authority of the Congress is always subject to the superior powers of the people to amend the constitution to change that opinion. That power lies in the majority of Congress and state legislatures and the people who could amend the constitution. Thus, nothing is "locked in stone" from majorities who would be determined to get their way either by congressional action or constitutional amendment. It just takes more time. It is helpful to remind ourselves of what is beyond current legislative power of Congress, if no constitutional amendment is offered to change the current situation:

1. Congress cannot act like the president or the courts or a state under separation of powers and federalism.
2. Congress cannot levy variable duties, imposts or excises.
3. Congress cannot enact variable naturalization or bankruptcy laws.
4. Congress cannot appropriate money for armies for a term longer than two years.

5. Congress cannot suspend the writ of habeas corpus except in rebellion or civil war.
6. Congress cannot enact a bill of attainder or ex post facto law.
7. Congress cannot tax or lay a duty on any articles exported from any state.
8. Congress cannot favor ports in one state over another.
9. Congress cannot grant titles of nobility.
10. Congress cannot allow any impeached or convicted person to continue to hold office.
11. Congress cannot declare punishment for treason to "wash corruption of blood, or forfeiture except during the life of the person attained."
12. Congress cannot create new states from old states without consent of the states concerned.
13. Congress cannot fail to protect each state from invasion or against domestic violence.
14. Congress cannot stop two thirds of the legislatures of the states from calling for a constitutional convention proposing amendments.
15. Congress shall make no law respecting an establishment of religion or prohibit the free exercise thereof.
16. Congress shall make no law abridging the freedom of speech.
17. Congress shall make no law abridging the freedom of the press.
18. Congress shall make no law abridging the right of the people to peaceably assemble.
19. Congress shall make no law abridging the right of the people to petition the government for a redress of grievances.

Having just ended above on the First Amendment to the Bill of Rights passed in 1791, there are, in the balance of the constitution and amendments, a larger list of other commands, by the people, for Congress to follow and by interpretation, the states through the Fourteenth Amendment. The point needs emphasis. *The United States Constitution defines powers, grants powers and limits powers, but it offers no tyrannical power to Congress, the President or the Supreme Court to do to Americans as it sees fit in anyway it sees fit.* Majority rule by Congress and rule by the Executive and the judicial branches all have limits until the Constitution's rules are changed. For inner liberty, this is just the beginning of protection for citizens from misguided majorities, run-away legislative majorities and eccentric leaders in courts or elsewhere.

Every state in the United States provides the same or similar protection to liberty from the state—to protect inner liberty. Thus, constitutions and bills of rights are the protectors of inner liberty from intrusion by majorities in legislative bodies of all kinds, at all levels of government.

It is important to keep in mind that inner liberty as freedom from the state is no guarantee of freedom from the persuasion of friends, enemies, families, churches, schools, press, TV, unions, private clubs, corporations, universities, strangers, political parties and other private sources of persuasion. Free speech to argue against foolishness in human thought and action is readily available in a free society. It is solely state-sanctioned authority that is limited and that is the key, not societal pressures—community arguments, religious arguments, moral and ethical arguments, philosophical and historical arguments against foolish ideas or foolish actions. The arsenal of persuasion beyond the state is great and growing with mass media.

Inner Liberty and Authenticity: To Thine Own Self Be True

Perhaps the best definition of inner liberty to date is offered by Charles Taylor in *The Ethics of Authenticity* (1992).[66] Taylor sees and articulates the truth about inner liberty or freedom from the state in his own way.

Taylor's work is a "work of retrieval" as he described what needs to be done to the ideal of authenticity:

In other words, instead of dismissing this culture altogether, or just endorsing it as it is, we ought to attempt to raise its practice by making more palpable to its participants what the ethic they subscribe to really involves.[67]

That is the thrust of his book—to understand the safety and dangers of such an ethic of self-directed freedom. Both the boosters and knockers of the culture of authenticity as he calls them are wrong because, as Taylor argued, we ought to be trying to lift the culture closer to its motivating ideal. The definition of the cultural mainstream in Western liberal society over the last 200 years is found in individualism and in what Taylor describes so clearly and beautifully to be the ideal of authenticity. But there are fraudulent and misguided impostors and quacks to threaten us.

First, to concentrate on the ideal of authenticity, Taylor offered his definition of what I have tried with great difficulty to describe as inner liberty: "Authenticity is itself an idea of freedom; it involves my finding the design of my life myself, against the demands of external conformity."[68] Taylor suggested that the philosopher Herder "put forward the idea that each of us has an original way of being human." Taylor continued:

This idea [of Herder] has entered very deep into modern consciousness. It is also new. Before the late eighteenth century no one thought that differences between human beings had this kind of moral significance. There is a certain way of being human that is *my* way. I am called upon to live my life in this way, and not in imitation of anyone else's. But this gives a new importance to being true to myself. If I am not, I miss the point of my life, I miss what being human is for *me*.[69]

The moral idea of authentic or genuine individualism that underlies Taylor's ideal of authenticity requires an inner voice, and each voice of each person has something to say on its own. Finding that voice is a life's work, a life time of education. But even self-determining freedom can degenerate morally into a degraded, absurd or trivialized form of choice, Taylor argued. Some evidence of this is found in statements commonly heard:

- "You should do your own thing."
- "You should find your own fulfillment."
- "It is impossible to argue about another person's values, we ought to mutually respect values of others."

Taylor described this weak view of authenticity that is found in soft relativism by arguing that

People are called upon to be true to themselves and to seek their own self-fulfillment. What this consists of, each must, in the last instance, determine for him- or herself. No one else can or should try to dictate its content.[70]

This subjective character of self-fulfillment Taylor believed to be a *profoundly mistaken* view of self-determining freedom. It fits with a view that a liberal society must be neutral on what constitutes the good life because "The good life is what each individual seeks, in his or her own way, and government would be lacking in impartiality, and thus in equal respect for all citizens, if it took sides on this question."[71] This example of soft relativism joins with moral subjectivism—"you cannot adjudicate moral disputes." Among soft relativism, narcissism and self-fulfillment Taylor finds the ideal of authenticity that he argues is *none* of the above. I conclude that this ideal of authenticity by Taylor is the modern core of inner liberty from the state and seeing it this way makes both national freedom and freedom within a state valid subjects of freedom that are connected to, but remote from, the idea of freedom from a state with its own lineage linked to authenticity. Taylor has achieved the most accurate analysis of the truth of the ideal of authenticity that exists so far, and in so doing, illuminates Mill's inner liberty and Kant's categorical imperatives.

Going Beyond the Constitution

The idea of inner liberty from a state revives the idea of there being a source of law in the reason of a single human being that Cicero called natural law. Perhaps out of an ideal of authenticity, Antigone buried her brother against King Creon's commands that were merely erroneous, earthly, state-driven demands of positive law from a person in power. Antigone was being true to the ideal of authenticity as she saw it. It was her inner voice. It was a superior moral idea to bury her dead brother. When one goes beyond the constitution for rights, then one is inevitably drawn toward the natural rights justifications inherent in the Declaration of Independence, the Bill of Rights, the United States Constitution and the "moral horizons" described by Taylor. The "higher law" of Edward S. Corwin is what lies behind a written constitution.[72]

In his own way Hadley Arkes in *Beyond the Constitution* (1990) argued for the principles of moral reasoning that stood in custom and common law before there was a written constitution, and this is quite parallel to Taylor's finding an ideal of authenticity developing in liberal thought for well over 200 years. But Taylor explained the idea of moral horizons more clearly than Arkes explained his laws of reason that do not need explanations. Faith alone is a weak reed in modern society. Arkes referred to the certain relativism or moral skepticism that exists, even in conservative ideas of law, that fights with the moral reasoning that has always been a tradition of natural law and natural rights. A liberal might argue the same way but would be embarrassed to acknowledge the link to natural rights because positive law thinking still has quite a hold on pragmatic American legal thoughts. Arkes makes clear that legal positivism and moral relativism have displaced natural rights in thinking in many of those who are aware of such distinctions.

It is obvious that inner liberty from the state, whether based on Taylor's ideal of authenticity or upon some older notions of natural law based on human reason that Arkes and others could identify, must be exercised against a background of intelligible choices—when one choice as opposed to another can be determined to be significant even superior. All choices are not equal, because as Taylor explained about moral subjectivism: "But this implicitly denies the existence of a preexisting horizon of significance, whereby some things are worthwhile and others are less so, and still others not at all, quite anterior to choice." [73] Anything chosen is not good and all right—it can only be judged in the light of an inescapable horizon as Taylor argued. The Nazi Keitel found this true of justice and national freedom as explained above. Taylor said self-creation is not "copping out, going with the flow or conforming with the masses." The chosen life as a moral ideal to be worthwhile—that is, a good life—cannot be allowed to become trivial and incoherent by following random subjectivity of choice. Slavery and torture of people is a choice not at all worthwhile or good by any reasonably humane universal standard. No one should have inner liberty to make such an evil choice, but we know some people may become immoral by their own choice. "Involuntary servitude" for crimes still exists in America. Only a common moral horizon of justice, equality and constitutional order can control the evil flowing from freedom of inner liberty to attempt harm to others by slavery and by torture.

The sense of freedom from a state, a nation or the United Nations revolves around the factors just considered in this third part of Chapter 6 devoted to offering an analysis of applications of freedom in its more refined definitions and in its interaction with other values. If successful in conveying the intended meaning and emphasis about the definition of liberty in modern America, then this chapter will have accomplished its purpose to illustrate clearly how and why freedom has three parts, and why and how freedom interacts with other values not only in paired ways but in combinations of ways, depending on the circumstances. Contingency of freedom is not a lessening of its value, it is a demonstration of the real power of freedom to drive us.

Chapter 7

Transformed Freedom and the Future

TO BE OR NOT TO BE FREE: WHAT IS THE QUESTION?

The question for the future of the American Dream of Freedom is not: Do Americans have too many freedoms? Neither is it: Do Americans have too few freedoms? The future questions should be framed around the three major aspects of freedom defined above: national freedom, freedom within the state and freedom from the state. The principal reason to justify this division is to clarify public debate, and, thereby, to reduce misunderstandings about any debate involving freedom in America. This change could be illustrated rather easily by reformulating the principal questions suggested by a more carefully developed understanding of transformed freedom.

A transformed freedom suggests that the following questions are examples of the real and better questions to ask about the state of liberty in America.

National Freedom

1. Do we have a solid national freedom on a global basis, and are we paying attention to it every day?
2. How are we nurturing the quality of our national freedom on a global basis among foreign governments and all multinational corporations?
3. Are we serious about national popular sovereignty and its link to national freedom?

Freedom Within the State

1. How do we nurture freedom within the state, within America and each of the states and territories by respecting limits of federal power and limits of corporate power? Do we respect separation of powers to protect liberty?
2. Is the state doing all that is possible to nurture the freedom of every citizen to vote, to hold office, and to foster representative democracy?

Freedom from the State

1. How well do agents of the state (elected and appointed) understand the outer limits of the power of government in a society called America?
2. Do citizens understand, debate, define and believe that there is a sphere of life where the state must leave citizens alone?
3. Do citizens in America understand and believe in our individual law-giving and law-making responsibilities to ourselves in zones of life where the state has no right to exist? Who is to teach them this ultimate responsibility of personhood?

Freedom and Other Values

The following questions and their opposites tie other values to liberty, and they could be framed for national freedom, freedom within the state and freedom from the state:

Justice—Do Americans know when justice must prevail over liberty and why?

Equality—Do Americans know when equality must prevail over liberty and why?

Authority, Order and Security—Do Americans know when authority, order and security must prevail over liberty and why?

Property—Do Americans know when the owner of private property should prevail over liberty and why?

Privacy—Do Americans know when the privacy of a citizen must prevail over liberty and why?

These sample questions are more carefully framed than the too few-too many framework that does not even distinguish among types of freedom. It is now possible to ask, in a more rational way, when justice must prevail over liberty in at least three different situations. That is, in national freedom, when must considerations of justice outweigh national liberty of Americans? When must considerations of justice outweigh freedom of Americans within the nation? Finally, when must considerations of justice outweigh the freedom from the state for Americans? Criminal codes do answer much of this quite thoroughly. This exercise of questions could go on for other significant values indicated above. The framework of questions could help the United Nations shape its inquiry into the human freedom index that it wishes to develop. Such a framework of analysis could be useful for development of more probing public discussion on television, in news media and in education at all levels from grade school to postgraduate study and adult education. There may be uses that have not been thought of yet.

The analytical questions are certainly better than telling people what their freedom consists of—frankly, we do not know the given combinations of circumstances to be faced by Americans now and in the future, nor do we know the possible aspects of freedom involved and the important values contending with freedom. I am arguing that almost everything is contingent in the field of freedom, but the fixed verities are very few under all circumstances and where all the desired values are at stake and in conflict.

SLAVERY

One such verity without contingency or conditions, and without Walter Lippmann's weasel words, cutting across all definitions of freedom is the belief finally reached about chattel slavery of human beings, that is, owning and selling people as one would sell a cow or horse. It is called slave trade. The Thirteenth Amendment to the United States Constitution reads:

Neither slavery nor involuntary servitude, except as a punishment for crime whereof the party shall have been duly convicted, shall exist within the United States, or any place subject to their jurisdiction.

The 38th Congress submitted this amendment to the states on February 1, 1865, and it was ratified rapidly by the states by December 8, 1865. This is the best example of an absolute freedom or liberty in America. No questions of property, justice, equality, order or privacy can channel this liberty to permit slavery, except as a punishment for crime.

President Abraham Lincoln in the famous Lincoln-Douglas debates on October 15, 1858, in Alton, Illinois, saw the eternal and universal nature of slavery saying it would remain an "eternal struggle" between right and wrong "throughout the world." Those are his very well chosen words. What is right is no slavery in any form—liberty belongs to all the people. Lincoln said in the debate:

The one is the common right of humanity and the other the divine right of kings. It is the same principle in whatever shape it develops itself. It is the same spirit that says, "You work and toil and earn bread, and I'll eat it." [Loud applause] No matter what shape it comes, whether from the mouth of a king who seeks to bestride the people of his own nation and live by the fruit of their labor or from one race of men as an apology for enslaving another race, it is the same tyrannical principle. [*Collected Works of Abraham Lincoln*, Roy A. Basler (ed.), 1953, Vol. III, 315]

For slavery, I cannot conceive of domestic and international circumstances that would define justice, property, equality, privacy or authority in such a way as to provide a right and reasonable justification of slavery in the future over the obvious need for national freedom, freedom within the state or freedom from the state with the sole exception of punishment for crimes. Western Civilization has proceeded so far along its course that human slavery is not a subject any longer of significant public discourse except for an occasional case of involuntary servitude. Although Jodi L. Jacobson at the World Watch Institute now reports upon a variety of forms of slavery in 1992, they lie outside of Western Civilization—in India, Pakistan, Thailand, Sudan, South Africa and the Philippines.[1] The reach of Western Civilization is not global in nature in so basic a matter as slavery of human beings, no matter how much we think it may be a *universal* value to stop slavery.

TRENDS, SPHERES AND TIME: THE STRUGGLES AHEAD

The truth about all forms of freedom is that they are dynamic, ever changing in nature. There are not fixed spheres where freedom exists for all time. There are spheres or parts of the world where freedom is more influential than other parts. There are times when freedom is more widespread than other times. But in the 20th century, and especially during the two world wars, many reasonable minds became convinced that freedom is properly conceived as a struggle—a perpetual fight that never ends for each human being until death. Victor Ehrenberg believed that the ancient Greeks saw freedom as a perpetual struggle, a thing to be earned. Charles Taylor is clearly of this same perspective:

In a sense, a genuinely free society can take as its self-description the slogan put forward in quite another sense by revolutionary movements like the Italian Red Brigades: *la lotta continua*—the struggle goes on—in fact, forever.[2]

LIMITS OF THE STATE: THE SPHERE OF PRIVATE FREEDOM

As I indicated at the outset of this book, the truth is that many Americans have an extraordinarily incomplete and inadequate approach toward defining freedom, even if it may be the preeminent value of Western Civilization. There must be perverse incentives to maintain such a state of affairs. Kammen notes that "With very few exceptions, Americans have not been inclined to undertake theoretical explications concerning liberty." [3] That may be changing with Adler's, Kammen's and Patterson's work on liberty which is found in a small stream of other books. The truth must be, for now, that we do not know whether any person, any government, or any private institution has too many or too few freedoms, especially in view of the confusion about the meaning of liberty that prevails today. For the most part, many Americans, when and if they think about freedom and liberty, are too superficial, too ideological, too lacking in intellectual persistence, too captured by a bill of rights and constitutional logic, too taken in by business, science and technology to see their own predicament over something they all supposedly treasure—freedom. I think it is fair to call this phenomenon—mass blindness focused primarily on liberty—inner liberty.

In 1859, John Stuart Mill opened *On Liberty* with these words by Wilhelm von Humboldt:

The grand, leading principle, towards which every argument unfolded in these pages directly converges, is the absolute and essential importance of human development in its richest diversity.
   Sphere and Duties of Government (1854) Wilhelm von Humboldt (translation).

We need to examine Mill's choice of Humboldt with a patient caring because the choice is striking. Wilhelm von Humboldt (1767-1835) was the source of Mill's quotation, and he was an eminent and highly regarded politician and educational thinker in Germany. He founded the University of Berlin. Mill considered the work of Humboldt vital and essential by citing specific parts of it in his essay. Humboldt wrote *Sphere and Duties of Government* in 1791-1792 when he was only twenty-four. His complete works were first published in 1852, posthumously by his brother, Alexander. It is clear that Mill found satisfaction in Humboldt's book on government. It is remarkable that the words and ideas in the German language, of a youthful German writer, published seventeen years after he died, would influence an Englishman of Mill's intellectual stature and age at fifty-three. This is a puzzle that Humboldt himself dispels. In a 1969 English edition of *Sphere and Duties of Government* by J. W. Burrow for Cambridge University Press, the new title in English is revised to *The Limits of State Action.* This edition begins with Humboldt's observation: "To discover to what end State institutions should be directed, and what limits should be set to their activity, is the design of the following pages." [4]

At the beginning Humboldt stated two main objects in framing a constitution:

1. To determine, for the nation in question, who shall govern, who shall be governed, and to arrange the actual working of the administration

2. To prescribe the exact sphere to which the government, once constructed, should extend or confine its operations[5]

Humboldt then observes:

The latter object [2 above], which more immediately affects the private life of the citizen, and more especially determines the limits of his free, spontaneous activity, is, strictly speaking, the true ultimate purpose; the former [1 above] is only a necessary means for arriving at this end. And yet, however, it is to the attainment of the first of these ends that man directs his most earnest attention; and this exclusive pursuit of one definite purpose is the way human activity usually manifests itself.[6]

Humboldt was right for us even today; we spend too much time on machinery of governing for goal number one, not enough on limits of goal number two. And when we hear anguished cries about freedom today, it is usually an inadequate answer to goal number two that the government, especially the national government, has no limit to what it can do. I attempted to dispel this falsehood by listing again the limits of congressional power given in the last chapter. We say that states in the United States of America are limited. How foolish this thinking about the federal government is for all aspects of freedom under almost any circumstances. How fearful a totalitarian ring this assertion of unlimited power has toward a person's freedom from the state. After forty years of Cold War, we may have forgotten extremely important priorities in this aspect of freedom. Excessive centralization of power may enhance national freedom, but it may also destroy freedom within the state, and it may destroy freedom from the state—the cherished inner liberty. The remains of the Cold War, I am certain, influences this myopic perspective.

The exact sphere to which the government should extend or confine its operations has a bearing on the degree of freedom that Americans believe they have as a birthright. If we fail to address this question, we will not get far in protection of freedom in all of its various meanings, under a variety of circumstances. One either believes there are limits to government worth discussing and having the government obey such limits, or one has totalitarianism on the mind as a guidepost. We discovered from Nazi Germany in 1940 that there is in some minds no logical end to the state. That is what totalitarianism means. The words of Albert Camus, quoted in Chapter 6, reinforce this understanding. Could it be that Humboldt, Camus, Learned Hand and Mill were addressing a world that still describes a central problem in America at the end of the 20th century? I think so even if we, as a nation, have given exceptional attention to the general subject of liberty without pausing to consider better ways to define freedom and how those definitions interact with other values we do treasure—equality, property, security, order, authority, privacy and justice.

LIMITS OF THE GIANT CORPORATION: FREEING AMERICA FROM CHIPS OFF THE BLOCK OF STATE SOVEREIGNTY

Philippa Strum in *Louis D. Brandeis: Justice for the People* (1984) observed certain concerns of Justice Brandeis about the "curse of bigness" in American life:

Throughout his adult life one of Brandeis's major concerns was bigness; a book of his collected papers was entitled *The Curse of Bigness*. Anything that ignored the limitations of human nature and the difficulty human beings experienced in ascertaining the most successful patterns of life was to be avoided. Above all, human beings had to be wary of the evil of bigness, in government as well as in business. For with their complex combination of creativity and limited intellect, human beings could create institutions that were too big for them: too big to monitor for efficiency and effectiveness, too big to assess for value or liability to society, too big to control.[7]

Apart from giant governments, the freedom of enterprise of multinational corporate giants in American society is not an inescapable price of civilized life, nor is it an evil in many cases that a nation should ignore if it values liberty in all its aspects. This point was made in Chapter 6 above. Justice Brandeis in 1933 in *Liggett v. Lee* said early in our history the right to incorporate businesses was *denied* by the states:

It was denied because of fear. Fear of encroachment upon liberties and opportunities of the individual. Fear of the subjection of labor to capital. Fear of monopoly. There was a sense of some insidious menace inherent in large aggregations of capital, particularly when held by corporations.[8]

The end of the 20th century is seeing a rebirth of such fears spawned by Fortune 500 corporations and multinational corporations. We do not have a modern legal jurisprudence to guide us although one may be evolving.[9] In Adolph Berle and Gardner Means work, *The Modern Corporation and Private Property* (1932) and in Thorstein Veblen's earlier *Absentee Ownership and Business Enterprise* (1923), there was reinforced the concurrent fears of Brandeis. Graef Crystal and William Greider reinforce these fears today in their own way. The results of marked concentration of individual wealth, the creation of extraordinary annual salaries in terms of millions of dollars, and growth of needless income disparities among citizens is one obvious result of the corporate giants which the fifty states have allowed to be created by their incorporation laws over the last 100 years. Furthermore, globalization of markets has launched domestic corporate giants into the international world without sufficient international, national or state control. An international corporate arrogance has grown too great. National freedom is jeopardized by new claims of corporate sovereignty that are asserted by people like Walter Wriston, former head of Citicorp. Freedom within a nation or state is put in peril by threats from giant corporations to take capital elsewhere in the world unless they are allowed to dominate political and social agendas of the people. Ultimately, popular sovereignty of 250 million American citizens is put in peril. Freedom of the fifty states in the United States is lessened; their sovereignty undermined when corporate giants beseech in Washington the Congress, the presidency and the Supreme Court with money and influence to build preemptive national federal controls over all of a citizen's life in the name of national and, now, international "free" markets. Finally, freedom from a state is imperiled by giant corporations and their pervasive and persuasive grants of money to media such as PBS public television and their ownership of mass media (NBC owned by GE) drowning out the voice of the people. William Greider would ask, "Who will tell the people of the betrayal of American democracy by corporate giants?" Attempts at thought control through advertising backed by the treasuries of Coca Cola, Budweiser, Ford, General Motors and hundreds of others is a threat to inner liberty, to freedom from the state or its modern-day surrogate—the great American corporation. This is an old problem of liberty for Americans to tackle anew. Ravi Batra in *The Myth of Free Trade* (1993) offered a solution: "We should break up large firms controlling more than 10 percent of market share in any industry and at the same time actively guard them from foreign competition."[10]

The idolatry of giantism in American society—that gigantic organizations are inescapably necessary—calls into play the antinomy of order and freedom, all which exceeds logic. As E. F. Schumacher in *Small Is Beautiful* (1973) said, "The centre can easily look after order: it is not so easy to look after freedom and creativity." [11] The curse of bigness that troubled Justice Brandeis early in the 20th century still finds expression late in the century in E. F. Schumacher's counseling of an overwhelming need for a human scale to living and working. It is economics, as if people mattered. The truth of crime and terrorism, genocide, breakdown, breakup, pollution and exhaustion is closing in on Americans. Giant corporations strain to exist and downsize. Civic debt is higher and higher. A myth of "free trade" haunts us. A renewed dedication to freedom in all three aspects defined in this book offers a new logic to solve the perpetual curse of bigness haunting Americans to the end of the 20th century. We ought to learn prudence and to know "when enough is enough." [12]

The approach toward freedom of Americans in this book should begin to free our thinking about the important central idea of liberty in our society. Thinking about human liberty in terms of national freedom, freedom within the state and freedom from the state is the beginning. Then asking oneself about the contingent nature of liberty as it touches on authority, order, security, justice, equality, property and privacy could open a new era in thinking more productively about desirable public policy in America toward business and government. Eternal vigilance, *la lotta continua*, perpetual alertness is demanded by liberty in America.

Appendix 1

The Human Freedom Index and HFI Ranking of Selected Countries

BOX 1.2

The human freedom index

The goal of human development is to increase people's choices. But for people to exercise their choices, they must enjoy freedom—cultural, social, economic and political.

The *World Human Rights Guide*, by Charles Humana, uses 40 indicators to measure freedom:

The right to
• travel in own country
• travel abroad
• peacefully associate and assemble
• teach ideas and receive information
• monitor human rights violations
• ethnic language

The freedom from
• forced or child labour
• compulsory work permits
• extra-judicial killings or "disappearances"
• torture or coercion
• capital punishment
• corporal punishment
• unlawful detention
• compulsory party or organization membership
• compulsory religion or state ideology in schools

• arts control
• political censorship of press
• censorship of mail or telephone-tapping

The freedom for
• peaceful political opposition
• multiparty elections by secret and universal ballot
• political and legal equality for women
• social and economic equality for women
• social and economic equality for ethnic minorities
• independent newspapers
• independent book publishing
• independent radio and television networks
• independent courts
• independent trade unions

The legal right to
• a nationality
• being considered innocent until proved guilty
• free legal aid when necessary and counsel of own choice
• open trial
• prompt trial
• freedom from police searches of home without a warrant

• freedom from arbitrary seizure of personal property

The personal right to
• interracial, interreligious or civil marriage
• equality of sexes during marriage and for divorce proceedings
• homosexuality between consenting adults
• practice any religion
• determine the number of one's children

Drawing on the 1985 data in the *World Human Rights Guide* and assigning a "one" to each freedom protected and a "zero" to each freedom violated, the country ranking in table 1.5 emerges. Clearly, this ranking for the human freedom index (HFI) needs updating. Adding recent information for only one of the 40 aspects of freedom—multiparty elections by secret and universal ballot—makes for many changes. Eighteen countries see their HFI improve.

The world today is a freer world. An updated human freedom index based on a limited number of observable and objectively measurable key indicators is more than overdue.

TABLE 1.5
HFI ranking of selected countries

Country total of freedoms, 1985		▲ Recent move towards greater freedom (multiparty elections held)
High freedom ranking (31-40)	25 Jamaica	8 Yugoslavia
38 Sweden	24 Ecuador	▲ 8 Chile
38 Denmark	23 Senegal	8 Kuwait
37 Netherlands	▲ 21 Panama	▲ 8 Algeria
36 Finland	21 Dominican Rep.	8 Zimbabwe
36 New Zealand	19 Israel	8 Kenya
36 Austria	▲ 18 Brazil	8 Cameroon
35 Norway	18 Bolivia	▲ 7 Hungary
35 France	16 Peru	7 Turkey
35 Germany, Fed. Rep. of	15 Mexico	7 Morocco
35 Belgium	14 Korea, Rep. of	7 Liberia
34 Canada	14 Colombia	▲ 7 Bangladesh
34 Switzerland	14 Thailand	▲ 6 German Dem. Rep.
33 USA	14 India	▲ 6 Czechoslovakia
33 Australia	14 Sierra Leone	6 Saudi Arabia
32 Japan	13 Nigeria	6 Mozambique
32 United Kingdom	▲ 13 Benin	5 Cuba
31 Greece	11 Singapore	5 Syrian Arab Rep.
31 Costa Rica	11 Sri Lanka	5 Korea, Dem. Rep. of
	11 Tunisia	5 Indonesia
Medium freedom ranking (11-30)	11 Egypt	5 Viet Nam
30 Portugal	11 Ghana	▲ 5 Pakistan
30 Papua New Guinea		5 Zaire
29 Italy	**Low freedom ranking (0-10)**	▲ 4 Bulgaria
29 Venezuela	▲ 10 Poland	▲ 3 USSR
27 Ireland	▲ 10 Paraguay	3 South Africa
26 Spain	▲ 10 Philippines	2 China
26 Hong Kong	10 Tanzania, U. Rep. of	2 Ethiopia
26 Botswana	9 Malaysia	▲ 1 Romania
25 Trinidad and Tobago	9 Zambia	1 Libyan Arab Jamahiriya
▲ 25 Argentina	▲ 9 Haiti	0 Iraq

Note: Ranking of countries with the same degree of freedom is done in accordance with HDI ranking.

Source: Human Development Report 1991 (New York: Oxford University Press, 1991)

Appendix 2

Federal Preemption Statutes—1790–1991

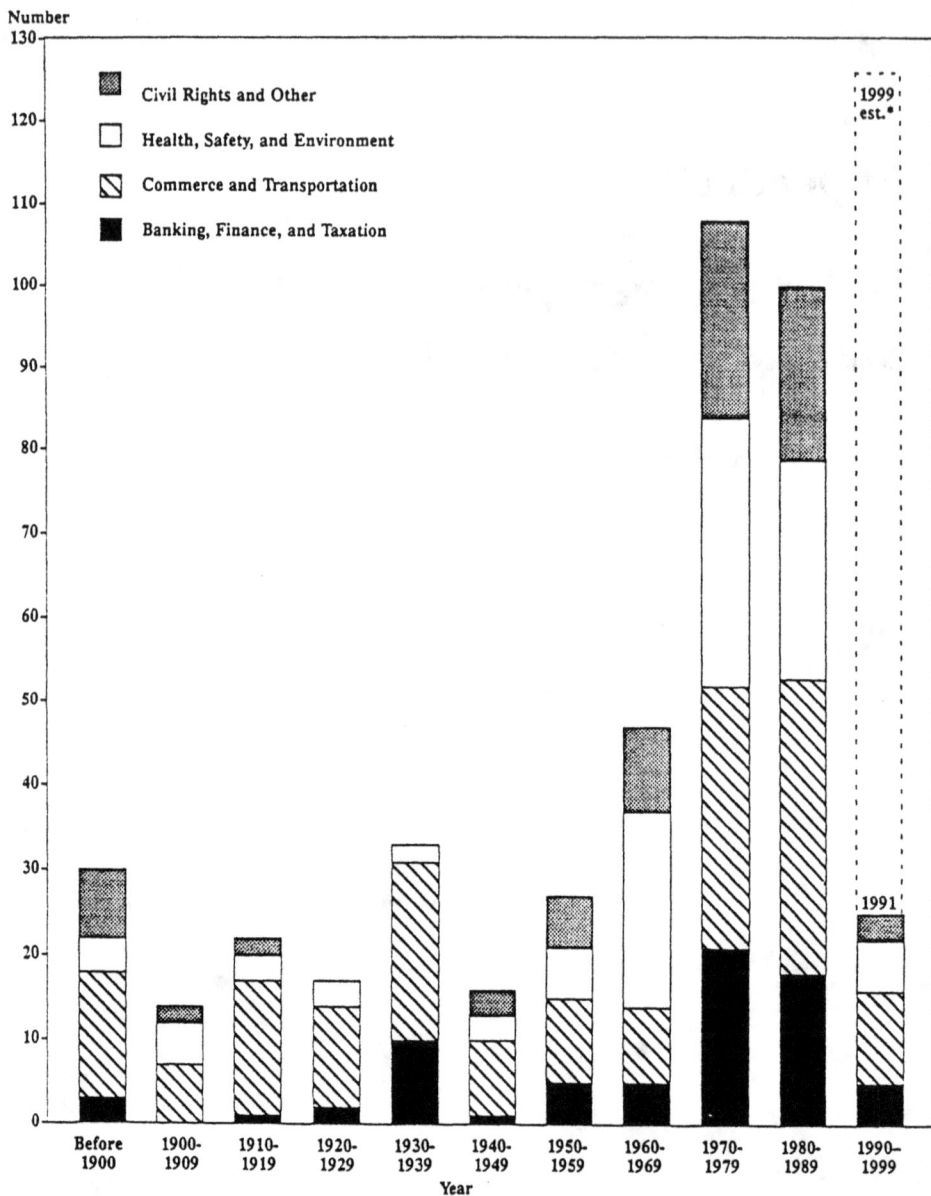

Figure 1
Number of Federal Preemption Statutes Enacted Per Decade: 1790-1991
(by date of enactment and purpose)

* The 1990-1991 rate was multiplied by 5 to estimate how many preemptions might be enacted during 1990-1999.

September 1992 ACIR Report—U.S. Advisory Commission on Intergovernmental Relations

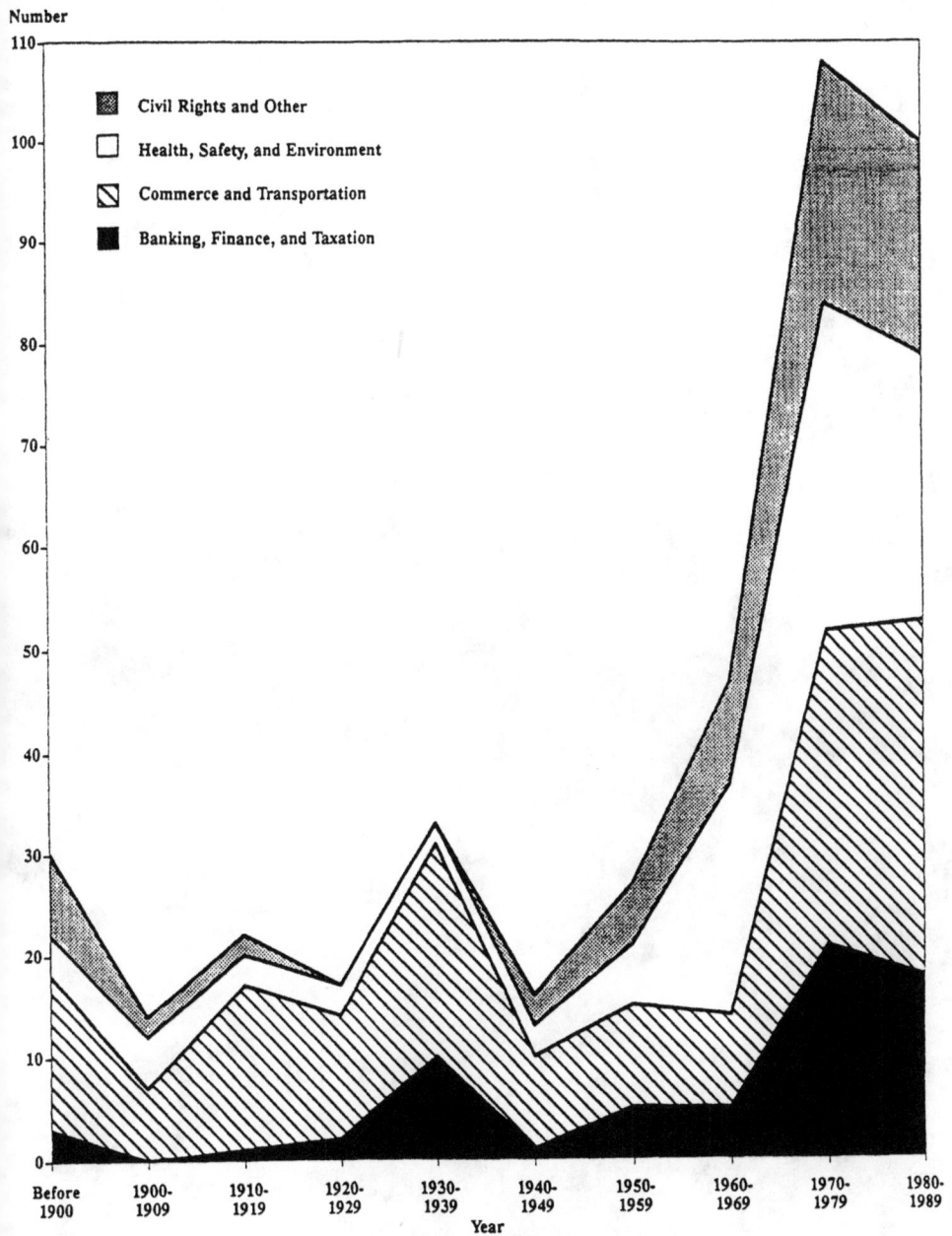

Figure 2
Number of Federal Preemption Statutes Enacted Per Decade: 1790-1989
(by date of enactment and purpose)

Number

Civil Rights and Other

Health, Safety, and Environment

Commerce and Transportation

Banking, Finance, and Taxation

Year

Before 1900 / 1900-1909 / 1910-1919 / 1920-1929 / 1930-1939 / 1940-1949 / 1950-1959 / 1960-1969 / 1970-1979 / 1980-1989

U.S. Advisory Commission on Intergovernmental Relations

131

Appendix 3

Translation of *Funeral Oration* by Pericles—431 B.C.

(34)   During the same winter the Athenians, in accordance with ancestral custom, conducted a funeral at public expense for those men who had first died in this war. The funeral rites are conducted in the following way: the bones of the departed are laid out for three days in a tent set up for that purpose, and each brings to his dead whatever offering he wishes. On the third day there is a procession; wagons carry cypress coffins, one for each tribe, and the bones of each man are in the coffin of his tribe, while one empty bier is draped over and carried for the missing who could not be found to take back. Whoever wishes, either citizen or stranger, takes part in the procession, and those women related to the dead are present to lament at the grave. The Athenians then place the coffins in the public tomb, which is located in the most beautiful area outside the city and in which they always bury those fallen in war, with the exception of those who died at Marathon; since they judged the excellence of those men to be extraordinary they placed their grave on the battlefield. But after the Athenians cover the dead with earth, a man chosen by the city, who appears by no means lacking in judgment and who is first in reputation, delivers to the people an appropriate eulogy, after which they depart. In this way they bury their fallen, and throughout the entire war, whenever occasion arose, they followed this custom. Now over the first men fallen in the war, Pericles, the son of Xanthippus, was chosen to speak. And when the appropriate moment came, he stepped forward from the tomb onto a platform built to a height that would allow him to be heard over as much of the crowd as possible and said the following:

[1]The *Funeral Oration* is presented in Thucydides' *History of the Peloponnesian Wars* in parts 2.35-2.46.

(35) "Many of those who have spoken here formerly have praised the man who added this speech to our custom on the grounds that it is proper and good that it be delivered at the burial of those who have died in war. But to me it would seem sufficient, when men proved themselves good by their actions, by action to have honors paid to them, such as those you have just now seen provided for this funeral by the state, and not to risk the credibility of many men's excellence in one man, according to how well or poorly he has spoken. Indeed it is difficult to speak with due measure in a case where scarcely even the appearance of truthfulness is securely established. For a well-informed and well-disposed listener would perhaps think that what has been presented falls short of what he wishes and knows, and a listener without experience, whenever he should hear of anything beyond his own nature, out of envy would think that there was some exaggeration. And indeed, praise spoken about others is bearable only to the extent to which each man thinks himself capable of doing whatever he hears about; but whatever exceeds, this means immediately envy and distrust. But since this practice has been sanctioned by our forefathers as proper to the occasion, I too, following the custom, must attempt to meet the wishes and expectations of each one of you as much as possible.

(36) "I shall begin with our ancestors, for it is not only just but especially fitting on such an occasion that this honor be given to them. For this land, in which the same people have always lived generation after generation, they handed down as a free country to our times by their courage and excellence. Those men are worthy of praise and even more so our fathers, for by laboring to add to the possessions they had inherited, they left to us, the present generation, the empire which we now possess. And we who are still for the most part in the prime of life have ourselves increased its power in many respects, and have provided for our city to completely as to make it supremely self-sufficient both in war and in peace. Now I shall pass over the actions in war by which each possession was acquired, whether we ourselves or our fathers zealously repelled the attacking enemy, barbarian or Greek, since I am unwilling to make a long speech in the presence of those who know. But from what kind of principles we have come to this point, with what kind of political institutions, and from what characteristic way of life our city has become great, this I will make clear before turning to the praise of these men. For I believe that in the present circumstances, to give such an account would not be inappropriate, and to hear it would be advantageous to the whole assembly of both citizens and strangers.

(37) "We have a form of government that does not emulate the laws of our neighbors; we ourselves are a paradigm for others rather than their

imitators. And while it is called a democracy because its management is in the hands not of the few but of the many, yet while all men have equality under the laws in regard to private differences, it is according to one's public worth, how each shows distinction in some activity, that a man is preferred in public affairs, preferred not by rank so much as through personal excellence. Nor again has poverty kept anyone back through the obscurity of his position, so long as he is able to do some good for the city.

"And as we manage our public affairs in a spirit of freedom, so too in regard to mutual suspicions arising from daily business, we do not become angry toward our neighbor if he does what he likes, nor do we put on annoyed looks, which though harmless are nonetheless painful to see. And while we conduct our private associations so as to avoid giving offense, in public affairs we do not transgress the laws, primarily through a reverent fear; we attend carefully to those individuals who are currently in office and to the laws, especially those laws set down for the assistance of the injured which, although unwritten, bring universally recognized disgrace on the transgressor.

(38) "Furthermore, we have provided the greatest number of opportunities for the mind's relaxation from work, by holding contests and sacrifices throughout the year and through the daily enjoyment of beautiful property and possessions, which drives away petty cares. Due to the greatness of our city, everything is brought to us from everywhere, and thus it happens that we are no less familiar with the enjoyment of our own goods than we are with the goods of other peoples.

(39) "Moreover, we differ from our enemies in our military training and practices in the following ways. We keep our city open to all, and never, by any official expulsion of foreigners, do we prevent anyone from learning or seeing anything which, if not concealed, might benefit an enemy. For we put our trust not so much in preparations and trickery as in the courageous spirit of action which comes from our very selves. And in regard to methods of education, while some seek to acquire courage through laborious training from early youth, we, without such restraints, go forth to meet equal dangers no less than they. And here is a proof of this: the Spartans attack our land not by themselves, but with all their allies; but when we, by ourselves, invade our neighbors' territory, we usually prevail, although fighting in a foreign land against men defending their own homes.

"In fact, no enemy has ever yet encountered the power of our combined forces, due to the requirements for maintaining our fleet and the wide-ranging deployment of our forces on land. But if ever an enemy engages a part of our forces anywhere, whenever they prevail over some of us, they boast that they have repelled us all, and whenever they are conquered, that they were overwhelmed by all of us together. And surely if we wish to face dangers with ready ease rather than laborious training and with a courage arising not so much from laws as from character, we gain an advantage in that we do not wear ourselves out beforehand by anticipating future hardships. Moreover, when we do come upon trouble, we show ourselves no less daring than those who are forever laboring away. In these respects and also in others ways our city is worthy of wonder.

(40) "For we love beauty with simplicity and wisdom without effeminacy. We use our wealth as an opportunity for action rather than for wordy boasting, and poverty is no shameful thing to confess—even if it were, it would not be more shameful than running away from work. To the same men belongs the care of both private and public affairs, and others, who have devoted themselves to private business, do not lack understanding of political matters. For we alone consider the man who takes no share in political concerns to be not aloof but useless. And whether we as a people are making decisions or giving a proposal serious thought, we do not believe that speech is harmful to action; what harms action is the failure to be instructed through speech before proceeding to do what is necessary. Indeed, we differ from others in this respect also, that we same men are daring in the highest degree and also most calculating about what we intend to undertake, while for others ignorance is courage and calculation produces hesitation. Yet those men would be rightly judged to be most powerful in spirit who have the clearest knowledge of the fearful and the pleasant and yet do not, because of these, turn away from dangers. And in respect to moral excellence we have always been unlike most men, for we win friends not by receiving but by conferring benefits. Indeed, the one who has conferred a favor is a surer friend, seeing that he preserves the debt of gratitude by his continued good will towards the one he benefited. But the one who owes a favor has his purpose blunted, since he knows that he will return the good deed not as a favor but as a debt. And we alone offer help fearlessly, not through a calculation of our advantage but in a confidence arising from our freedom.

(41) "In short, I say that our city in all its parts is the education of Greece, and it seems to me that among us one and the same man in his own person, shows his self-sufficiency in the most varied situations and with the greatest grace and versatility. That this is not a mere boastful display of words for the occasion but the truth born out by actions, the very power of our city demonstrates, a power which we acquired from our characteristic way of life. For our city alone among its contemporaries proves itself in a crisis to be even more powerful than what is said about it, and it alone

neither causes any irritation for an attacking enemy because of the character of the men who defeat him nor gives any reason for criticism to a subject ally on the grounds that he is ruled by unworthy men. Our power has been demonstrated by very clear proofs, and is in no way indeed without witnesses; accordingly we will be the object of wonder for the present and future generations. And we have no need of a Homer to praise us or of any other poet, whose verse will give momentary pleasure but whose conjectures about what was actually done will be injured by the truth. Rather, we have forced all seas and lands to become accessible to our daring and we have settled everywhere eternal memorials of our injuries and benefits. For such a city, then, did these men nobly fight and die, thinking it right not to be deprived of it; and it is right that everyone they left behind desire to labor on its behalf.

(42) "For this reason I have lengthened my speech about our city, for I wished to teach you that this contest does not carry equal risks for us and for those who do not have our advantages in like degree, and at the same time with such proofs to establish clearly the praiseworthiness of those about whom I now speak. Indeed the greatest part of that praise has already been spoken, since the qualities of our city which I celebrated have been adorned by the virtuous deeds of these men and men like them; and it could not be said of many Greeks, as it can of these, that the account of their excellences equally matched their deeds. And it seems to me that their end clearly reveals the true virtue of a man, whether by first disclosing it or by giving its last confirmation. Even in the case of some men who were in other ways less than perfect, it is just to put above everything else the manly courage they displayed in wars for the sake of their country, since they blotted out evil with good and they gave more help by acting for the common cause than they inflicted injury by their private actions. But of these men here, neither did any of them become soft and weak by preferring the continued enjoyment of wealth, nor did any put off the terrible day in hopes of some day escaping poverty and becoming rich. Rather, because they understood that vengeance on one's enemies was more desirable than the possession or acquisition of wealth, and because they believed that of all dangers this was the most noble, they were willing in such danger to avenge themselves on their enemies and let go thoughts of wealth, turning in hope to the uncertainty of future success while in action resolving to rely on themselves in what was before their eyes. In this struggle, because they thought it right to defend and suffer rather than give in and be saved, they fled from the shameful word "coward" and put their very bodies on the line in action; and in the briefest moment of fate, at the height of glory, not of fear, they departed.

(43) "Thus these men proved themselves in a manner worthy of the city. But you who remain, while you should pray for a spirit more secure from danger, you should resolve that it be in no way less daring against the enemy. And do not examine the advantage of this by speeches alone, an advantage about which anyone could speak at length, enumerating to you, who know no less than he, how many benefits there are in repelling the enemy; but rather actively fix your gaze from day to day on the power of the city and become its lovers. And when it appears great to you, keep in mind that these men acquired its powers by daring, by knowing what was needed, and by allowing shame to guide them in action, and that if they ever failed in any attempt, at least they did not think it right to deprive the city of their virtue but freely offered to it their most noble sacrifice. For they gave their lives for the common good and received for themselves an ageless glory and a most illustrious tomb, not that in which they are laid but the one in which their glory remains forever celebrated on every occasion for inspired word and deed. For all the world is the tomb of famous men, and not only does their epitaph appear on monuments in their own land, but also in lands not their own there lives within each man their unwritten memorial, engraved on the mind, not on any work of art. Do you, therefore, take these men now as your rivals and, judging that happiness depends on freedom and freedom on courage, do not pay too much attention to the dangers of war. For it is not those in bad straits who have just cause for lavishly risking their lives, since they have not hope of any change from bad to good, but rather those men, if they live, are threatened with the opposite reversal, and those men to whom it makes the greatest difference if they fail. For it is more painful, at least to a man of spirit, to suffer misfortune along with more weakness than to suffer death, which is unfelt when accompanied by strength and hope for a common good.

(44) "For this reason I do not commiserate with the parents of these men (however many of you are present), but rather I will try to console them. For they know that they have grown up amid the twists and turns of events. Accordingly this is good fortune: whenever men are allotted, as these men now, a most glorious end—and you a most glorious grief—and when life was measured out to them equally for happiness and for making a good end. It is difficult, I know, to persuade you of this, for only too often will you have reminders of your loss in other men's good fortunes, which you yourselves once enjoyed; and grief is felt not over goods which a man is deprived of before experiencing, but which are stolen from him after he has become accustomed to them. But you should bear up in the hopes of more children, you who are still of an age to have them; for children born afterwards will cause forgetfulness of those who are not more for some families, while for the city they will provide a double advantage: it will not

be berefit and it will be secure. For men are not able to deliberate in any fair or just way if they do not share equally the risk of exposing their own children to dangers. As for those of you who have already passed your prime, consider as a gain the greater part of your life in which you enjoyed good fortune, and also that what remains will be brief; and let the fame of these men lighten your sorrow. For love of honor is alone ageless, and in the useless part of old age it is not so much profit, as some say, that delights a man but being honored.

(45) "And as for those of you here who are sons or brothers of these men, I see that your contest with them will be great (for everyone is accustomed to praise the dead); even with the highest virtues you would scarcely be judged to be, not equal, but a little less than they. For envy is felt against the living due to rivalry, while what is no longer in the way is honored with noncompetitive good will. But if I am to make some mention of womanly excellence, for those of you who will now be widows, I will express everything in a brief admonition. If you do not fall short of the nature which belongs to you, there will be great glory for you and also for her whose virtues or faults are least talked about among men.

(46) "I have now for my part spoken what appropriate words I had in compliance with the law, and those who are being buried have already been honored in part by our actions here today. In addition, the city will henceforth raise their children at public expense until they reach eighteen, thus offering to these men and to those left behind a victory crown of great value in such contests as these. For where the greatest prizes for excellence are offered, there the city if managed by the best men. But now, each of you, lament your own and depart."

Translator's Note: In the winter of 431 B.C., Pericles delivered his *Funeral Oration* for the Athenians who had died during the first year of the war between Athens and Sparta and their allies. It appears in Book II of Thucydides' *History of the Peloponnesian War*, after the historian's account of the debates and conflicts which led to the outbreak of war and almost immediately before his description of the great plague which descended on the Athenians in the second year of the war. The glorious vision of Athens and the Athenian character was meant to be read in conjunction with Thucydides' description of the disintegration of political and moral order during the plague. There are several translations of Thucydides' history. Perhaps one of the most available is Rex Warner's *Thucydides: The Peloponnesian War* (New York, revised with a new introduction and appendixes in 1972) published by Penguin Books. Those interested in the character and leadership of Pericles may wish to read the *Life of Pericles* by the ancient Greek biographer Plutarch. For a recent evaluation of the statesman, see D. Kagan's *Pericles of Athens and the Birth of Democracy* (New York: Free Press, 1991). W. Robert Connor's *Thucydides* (Princeton, 1984), and H. Rawlings' *The Structure of Thucydides' History* (Princeton, 1981) offer excellent discussions of both the form and content of Thucydides' work.

C. W. Kalkavage
January 24, 1994

Notes

INTRODUCTION

1.   Orlando Patterson, *Freedom,* vol. I, *Freedom in the Making of Western Culture* (New York: Basic Books, 1991), preface xi.

2.   Ibid., x.

3.   Ibid., xi.

4.   Michael Kammen, *Spheres of Liberty* (Madison, WI: University of Wisconsin Press, 1986), 172.

5.   Mortimer J. Adler, *The Idea of Freedom* (Garden City, NJ: Doubleday and Co., 1961), 2:5.

6.   Ibid., 2:6.

7.   Ibid., 2:6,7.

8.   Ibid., 2:8.

9.   Ibid., 2:10.

10.   John Stuart Mill, *On Liberty,* ed. E. Rapaport (Indianapolis: Hackett Publishing Co., Inc., 1859, 1978 Edition), 113.

11.   Stuart M. Speiser, *Lawyers and the American Dream* (New York: M. Evans & Co., 1993) offers a contrasting and more widely accepted definition of the American Dream with a positive outlook.

12.   Compare sick societies described by Robert B. Edgerton, *Sick Societies, Challenging the Myth of Primitive Harmony* (New York: Free Press, 1992).

CHAPTER 1

1.   See *The MOCA Contemporary,* vol. 1, no. 6 (August/September 1992), 6.

2.   The arguments of feminine equality and other rights are reaching significant levels of articulation by capable advocates. See Deborah L. Rhode, *Justice and Gender, Sex Discrimination and the Law* (Cambridge, MA: Harvard University Press, 1989); Naomi Wolf, *Fire with Fire: The New Female Power and How It will Change the 21st Century* (New York: Random House, 1993); and Catherine A. MacKinnon, *Toward a Feminist Theory of the State* (Cambridge, MA: Harvard University Press, 1989).

3.   Joseph P. Shapiro, *No Pity: People with Disabilities Forging a New Civil Rights Movement* (New York: Times Books, 1993).

CHAPTER 2

1.   William A. Donohue, *The New Freedom* (New Brunswick, NJ: Transaction Publishers, 1990), 26.

2.   Graef S. Crystal, *In Search of Excess: The Overcompensation of American Executives* (New York: W. W. Norton & Co., 1991).

3.   John Stuart Mill, *On Liberty*, ed. E. Rapaport, 1978 edition (Indianapolis: Hackett Publishing Co., Inc., 1859), 58.

4.   Ibid., 9.

5.   Ibid., 93.

6.   Ibid., 97.

7.   Ibid., 106-107.

8.   Bill Clinton and Al Gore, *Putting People First* (New York: Times Books, 1992), 51.

9.   Amitai Etzioni, *The Spirit of Community* (New York: Crown Publishers, Inc., 1993), 54-88.

10.   Charles Taylor, *The Ethics of Authenticity* (Cambridge, MA: Harvard University Press, 1992), 14.

CHAPTER 3

1.   Karl Popper, "Knowledge: Subjective VERSUS Objective," (1967) in *Popper Selections*, ed. David Miller (Princeton, NJ: Princeton University Press, 1985). World I is the natural physical world; World II is a metaphysical and World III is a manmade product of the interaction of World I and World II.

2.   Hannah Arendt, *The Origins of Totalitarianism* (San Diego, CA: Harcourt Brace Jovanovich, 1951).

3.   United Nations Development Programme (UNDP), *Human Development Report 1991* (New York: Oxford University Press, 1991), 19.

4.   Paul L. Murphy, *World War I and the Origin of Civil Liberties in the United States* (New York: W. W. Norton & Co., 1979), 210-211.

5.   Samuel Walker, *In Defense of American Liberties: A History of the ACLU* (New York: Oxford University Press, 1990).

6.   Murphy, *World War I*, 10.

7.   Ira Glasser, *Visions of Liberty: The Bill of Rights for All Americans* (New York: Arcade Publishing, 1991).

8.   Kevin Phillips, *The Politics of Rich and Poor: Wealth and the American Electorate in the Reagan Aftermath* (New York: Random House, 1990).

9.   *Schmerber v. California*, 384 U.S. 757 (1966).

CHAPTER 4

1.   United Nations Development Programme (UNDP), *Human Development Report 1991* (New York: Oxford University Press, 1991), iii.

2.   Charles Humana, *World Human Rights Guide* (New York: Fact on File Publications, 1986).

3.   Paul Lewis, "UN Index on Freedom Enrages Third World," *New York Times*, June 23, 1991, 11.

4.   United Nations Development Programme, 98.

5.   United Nations, World Conference on Human Rights, *The Vienna Declaration and Programme of Action* (UN Department of Public Information, 1993).

6.   For a follow-on exposition of the flavor of continuing disagreements on universality of human rights, see Bilahari Kausikan, "Asia's Different Standard," *Foreign Policy* 92 (fall, 1993): 24-41 and Aryeh Neier, "Asia's Unacceptable Standard," *Foreign Policy* 92 (fall, 1993): 42-51. Social rights and economic rights are included in the UN idea of human rights that encompasses political and civil rights as well. The massive wave of books and articles on human rights in the last 10 years is too great to summarize here. See, for example, Louis Henkin and John L. Hargrove (Editors), *Human Rights: An Agenda for the Next Century* (Washington, D.C.: The American Society of International Law, 1994) and Richard P. Claude and Burns H. Weston (Editors), *Human Rights in the World Community: Issues and Action* (2nd Edition) (Philadelphia: University of Pennsylvania Press, 1992).

7.   John Stuart Mill, *On Liberty*, ed. E. Rapaport (Indianapolis: Hackett Publishing Co., Inc., 1859), 103.

8.   Stephen C. Halpern, *The Future of Our Liberties* (Westport, CT: Greenwood Press, 1982), 14.

CHAPTER 5

1. Karl Popper, "Indeterminism and Human Freedom," (1965) in *Popper Selections*, ed. David Miller (Princeton, NJ: Princeton University Press, 1985).

2. Isaiah Berlin, Four Essays on Liberty (London: Oxford University Press, 1969), 121-122.

3. Ibid., 122.

4. Richard N. Current, ed., *The Political Thought of Abraham Lincoln* (New York: Macmillan Publishing Co., 1967), 329.

5. Mark E. Neely, Jr., *The Fate of Liberty* (New York: Oxford University Press, 1991), 235.

6. C. S. Lewis, *Studies in Words* (London: Cambridge University Press, 1967), 7.

7. Ibid., 111-132.

8. Ibid., 112.

9. Ibid., 113.

10. Ibid., 115.

11. Ibid., 125.

12. Harold J. Berman, *Law and Revolution: The Formation of Western Legal Tradition* (Cambridge, MA: Harvard University Press, 1983), 320.

13. Herbert J. Muller, *Freedom in the Ancient World* (New York: Harper and Brothers, 1961), 145-194. See more about Muller in the next chapter.

14. Max Pohlenz, *Freedom in Greek Life and Thought* (Dordrecht, Holland: D. Reidel Publishing, 1966), 162.

15. Jacques Barzun, *The Culture We Deserve* (Middletown, CT: Wesleyan University Press, 1989), 169-171.

16. Ibid., 170.

17. Cynthia Farrar, *The Origins of Democratic Thinking* (Cambridge: Cambridge University Press, 1988), 104.

18. Victor Ehrenberg, *Man, State and Deity* (London: Methuen & Co., Ltd., 1974), 22-23.

19. *Trop v. Dulles, 356* U.S. *86* (1958).

20. Ehrenberg, *Man, State and Deity*, 20.

21. See Note 1, Chapter 3.

22. Kammen, *Spheres of Liberty: Changing Perceptions of Liberty in American Culture* (Madison, WI: University of Wisconsin Press), 172.

23. On April 8, 1952, President Harry Truman by Executive Order seized some of the private steel mills in the case that limited his power to do this, *Youngstown Sheet and Tube Co. v. Sawyer, 343* U.S. *579* (1952), decided June 2, 1952. The president unconstitutionally tried to exercise legislative power in the seizure, the Court ruled. See also Mavea Marcus, *Truman and the Steel Seizure Case: The Limits of Presidential Power* (New York:

Columbia University Press, 1977). David McCullough, in his 1992 biography titled, *Truman* (New York: Simon & Schuster, 1992), called the erroneous decision "one of the boldest, most controversial decisions of his Presidency." (896 et seq.).

The well-known economist Robert Heilbroner stated the link between economic order and social order this way: "Capitalism itself thus appears to be a social order that is both the embodiment and expression of freedom." See Robert Heilbroner, *21st Century Capitalism* (New York: W. W. Norton & Co., 1993), 73. But, "the most pressing problems of our coming century— namely, the internationalization of production and the globalization of our ecological encounter," (160) identified by Heilbroner as the most pressing are not resolved well by capitalism—clearly inadequate to the task in his view. There are many reasons for this that he suggests.

24. David A. Elder, *The Law of Privacy* (Deerfield, IL: Clark, Boardman and Callaghan, 1991).

CHAPTER 6

1. Martin Tolchin and Susan J. Tolchin, *Selling Our Security: The Erosion of America's Assets* (New York: Alfred A. Knopf, 1992).

2. See Bibliography for detailed list.

3. Herbert J. Muller, *Freedom in the Modern World* (New York: Harper & Row, 1966), xii.

4. Ibid., 516-517.

5. Ibid., 520.

6. Ibid., 528.

7. James MacGregor Burns, *The Vineyard of Liberty* (New York: Alfred A. Knopf, 1982), 62.

8. James MacGregor Burns, *The Crosswinds of Freedom*, (New York: Alfred A. Knopf, 1989), 679.

9. Victor Ehrenberg, *Man, State and Deity* (London: Methuen & Co., Ltd., 1974), 23.

10. Jacques Barzun in *The Culture We Deserve* (Middletown, CT: Wesleyan University Press, 1989) remarked: "Indeed, the only political ISM surviving in full strength from the past is Nationalism. This was partly to be expected from the liberation of so many colonies simultaneously, beginning in the 1920s. But this Nationalism differs from the old in two remarkable ways: it is not patriotic and it does not want to absorb and assimilate. On the contrary, it wants to shrink and secede, to limit its control to its own small group of like-minded we-ourselves-alone. It is in that sense racist, particularist, sectarian, minority-inspired. In truth, it flourishes as an expression of the antinomian passion which is the deepest

drive of the age" (169). This is a stunning observation about separatism. See also, Robert B. Edgerton, *Sick Societies* (New York: Free Press, 1992), 208-209 and Michael Ignatieff, *Blood and Belonging* (New York: Farrar, Straus and Giroux, 1993).

11.   Telford Taylor, *The Anatomy of the Nuremberg Trials* (New York: Alfred A. Knopf, 1992), 537.

12.   William Styron, *Darkness Visible* (New York: Random House, 1990), 24.

13.   Ibid., 21.

14.   Albert Camus, *Resistance, Rebellion, and Death*, trans. Justin O'Brien (New York: Alfred A. Knopf, 1961).

15.   Ibid., 27.

16.   Ibid., 36-37.

17.   Ibid., 247.

18.   Ibid., 247-248.

19.   Walter Lippmann, *Liberty and the News* (New York: Harcourt, Brace and Howe, 1920), 26.

20.   Learned Hand, *The Spirit of Liberty* (New York: Alfred A. Knopf, 1953), 189-190.   Irving Dillard Collection and Edition, Second Edition enlarged.   See Gerald Gunther, *Learned Hand, the Man and the Judge* (New York: Alfred A. Knopf, 1994), 547-552, 639-643.

21.   Lewis H. Lapham, *The Wish for Kings* (New York: Grove Press, 1993), 184.

22.   Ibid., 185.

23.   Ibid., 189.

24.   Gerry Spence, *From Freedom to Slavery* (New York: St. Martin's Press, 1993), 151.

25.   Ibid., 165-166.

26.   Michael Kammen, *Sovereignty and Liberty: Constitutional Discourse in American Culture* (Madison, WI: University of Wisconsin Press, 1988), 3.

27.   Kammen, *Spheres of Liberty: Changing Perceptions of Liberty in American Culture* (Madison, WI: Univeristy of Wisconsin Press, 1986), 151.

28.   Kammen, *Spheres of Liberty*, 155.

29.   James MacGregor Burns, *The Crosswinds of Freedom*, (New York: Alfred A. Knopf, 1989), 190.

30.   Graef S. Crystal, *In Search of Excess: The Overcompensation of American Executives* (New York: W. W. Norton & Co., 1991), 205.   Derek Bok, *The Cost of Talent, How Professionals and Executives Are Paid and How It Affects America* (New York: Free Press, 1993).

31.   Edwin H. Sutherland, *White Collar Crime: The Uncut Version* (New Haven: Yale University Press, 1983), 190.   Original edition 1949 by Dryden Press.

32.   Ibid., 191.

33. Ibid., 191.

34. Bill Clinton and Al Gore, *Putting People First* (New York: Times Books, 1992), 67.

35. William Greider, *Who Will Tell the People: The Betrayal of American Democracy* (New York: Simon & Schuster, 1992), 402.

36. Ibid., 401.

37. Tolchin, *Selling Our Security*, 202.

38. Ralph Nader, William Greider et al., *The Case Against Free Trade: GATT, NAFTA and the Globalization of Corporate Power* (San Francisco, Earth Island Press, 1993). See Thomas B. Edsall, "Issue Has Aroused the Left," *Washington Post*, November 8, 1993, 1, 10-11. The economist Ravi Batra in *The Myth of Free Trade, A Plan for American Economic Revival* (New York: Charles Scribner's Sons, 1993) opens the door to a stuffy subject.

39. Walter B. Wriston, *The Twilight of Sovereignty: How the Information Revolution Is Transforming Our World* (New York: Charles Scribner's Sons, 1992), 11. Compare an earlier well-known work, Richard J. Barnet and Ronald E. Müller, *Global Reach, The Power of Multinational Corporations* (New York: Simon & Schuster, 1974).

40. Ibid., 10.

41. Ibid., 16.

42. Ibid., xii, xiii.

43. For those who wish to pursue the origins, history and development of sovereignty in more depth, especially as it relates to liberty, see Michael Kammen, *Sovereignty and Liberty: Constitutional Discourse in American Culture* (Madison, WI: University of Wisconsin Press, 1988). Another perspective on sovereignty is found in Joseph A. Camilleri and Jim Falk, *The End of Sovereignty? The Politics of a Shrinking and Fragmenting World* (Hants, England: Edward Elgar Publishing Ltd., 1992). For a more extensive historical treatment of sovereignty, see Benjamin Constant, *Political Writings* (Cambridge: Cambridge University Press, 1988), 175; Charles E. Merriam, *History of the Theory of Sovereignty Since Rousseau* (New York: AMS Press, Inc., 1968—reprint of edition of 1900); Jean Bodin, *On Sovereignty* (Cambridge: Cambridge University Press, 1992); and Francis H. Hinsley, *Sovereignty* (New York: Basic Books, 1966). Not only sovereignty, but "free trade" and "capitalism" are problematic for liberty and freedom of a nation.

The founder and systematizer of capitalist economics, Adam Smith (1723-1790) is misused by many according to Jerry Z. Muller, *Adam Smith In His Time and Ours* (New York: Free Press, 1993). Muller stated:

Those who are most likely to cite Smith's authority often misunderstand the substance of his thought. His name is evoked by those who claim that the public good springs automatically out of the pursuit of self-interest, who regard government as the enemy of liberty, and who cite Smith's principal [principle] of "natural liberty" to defend the legalization of everything from pornography to guns to hard drugs. Many of those who style themselves Smithians substitute what they believe him to have said for that he actually said. (2)

Muller thinks that Smith wrote *The Wealth of Nations* to encourage legislators to resist political pressures of economic groups to advance their agendas. Since Smith's time, adding representative democracy, labor unions, a thriving, large, middle-class, and a well-educated society to a commercial society transforms in today's world the economic self-interest of business to major, but narrower, political influence. Political action committees are concrete evidence of Muller's views. Debates over the meaning of free trade must be recast today in a wider different society. See Richard F. Teichgraeber, *"Free Trade" and Moral Philosophy: Rethinking the Sources of Adam Smith's* Wealth of Nations (Durham, NC: Duke University Press, 1986) and Robert Heilbroner and Lester Thurow, *Economics Explained* (New York: Simon & Schuster, 1944) 195-206 and 239-240.

44.   Martin Ostwald, *From Popular Sovereignty to the Sovereignty of Law: Law, Society, and Politics in Fifth-Century Athens* (Berkeley, CA: University of California Press, 1986).

45.   Victor Ehrenberg, *Man, State and Deity* (London: Methuen & Co., Ltd., 1974), 28.

46.   Ibid., 27.

47.   Michael Kammen, *Spheres of Liberty*, 38-39.

48.   Ibid., 39.

49.   Ibid., 17.

50.   Arthur M. Schlesinger, Jr., *The Disuniting of America* (New York: W. W. Norton & Co., 1992), 134. See also, Arlene W. Saxonhouse, *Fear of Diversity, The Birth of Political Science in Ancient Greek Thought* (Chicago: University of Chicago Press, 1992) and Robert Hughes, *Culture of Complaint, The Fraying of America* (New York: Oxford University Press, 1993), 81-152.

51.   See Samuel H. Beer, *To Make a Nation, The Rediscovery of American Federalism* (Cambridge, MA: Belknap Press of Harvard University, 1993), 386-388.

52.   Arthur T. Vanderbilt, *The Doctrine of the Separation of Powers and Its Present Day Significance* (Lincoln, NE: University of Nebraska Press, 1953), 143-144. And see David J. Saari, "Separation of Powers, Judicial Impartiality and Judicial Independence: Primary Goals of Court Management Education" in Chapter 7, *Handbook of Court Administration and Management*, ed. Steven W. Hays and Cole B. Graham, Jr. (New York: Marcel Dekker, Inc., 1993), 141-182. For a superb analysis of modern tyranny see Daniel Chirot, *Modern Tyrants* (New York: Free Press, 1994).

53. United States Advisory Commission on Intergovernmental Relations, *A Commission Report, Federal Statutory Preemption of State and Local Authority: History, Inventory and Issues*, Washington, D.C., September 1992, page v. See also ACIR (July 1993), *Federal Regulation of State and Local Governments*.

54. Seven hundred years of Swiss federalism are noted by Max Frenkel, "The Communal Basis of Swiss Liberty," *Publius: The Journal of Federalism*, 23 (Spring 1993), 61-70. That experience contrasts with "The State of American Federalism 1992-1993," *Publius: The Journal of Federalism*, 23 (Summer 1993), 1-22. American federalism needs attention. See Samuel H. Beer, *To Make a Nation: The Rediscovery of American Federalism* (Cambridge, MA: Belknap Press of Harvard University, 1993) and David Schoenbrod, *Power Without Responsibility: How Congress Abuses the People Through Delegation* (New Haven, CT: Yale University Press, 1993).

55. John Stuart Mill, *On Liberty*, ed. E. Rapaport (Indianapolis: Hackett Publishing Co., Inc., 1859), 1.

56. Victor Ehrenberg, *Man, State and Deity*, 33.

57. Ibid., 34.

58. Ibid., 28.

59. Donald Kagan, *Pericles of Athens and the Birth of Democracy* (New York: Free Press, 1991), 146-147.

60. Ibid., 145-150.

61. Ibid., 147. See also Bernard Williams, *Shame and Necessity* (Berkeley: University of California Press, 1993) for relevance of ancient Greek ethical life.

62. Hand, *The Spirit of Liberty*, 152.

63. Ibid., 153.

64. Kammen, *Spheres of Liberty*, 129-172.

65. *Meyer v. Nebraska*, 262 U.S. 390 (1923).

66. Charles Taylor, *The Ethics of Authenticity* (Cambridge, MA: Harvard University Press, 1992).

67. Ibid., 72.

68. Ibid., 67-68.

69. Ibid., 28-29. Compare this statement of Taylor with the discussion in the case of *Planned Parenthood of Southeastern Pennsylvania v. Robert R. Casey* in Chapter 4 of this book. The Supreme Court majority stated,

At the heart of liberty is the right to define one's own concept of existence, of meaning, of the universe, and of the mystery of human life. Beliefs about these matters could not define the attributes personhood were they formed under compulsion of the state.

These statements are beginning to sound as if the ideal of authenticity is lodged into constitutional law and the definition of liberty in the United States.

70.   Ibid., 14.

71.   Ibid., 18.

72.   Edward S. Corwin, *The Higher Law Background of American Constitutional Law* (Ithaca, NY: Cornell University Press, 1929).

73.   Charles Taylor, *The Ethics of Authenticity*, 38. See Bernard Carnois, *The Coherence of Kant's Doctrine of Freedom* (Chicago: University of Chicago Press, 1987).

CHAPTER 7

1.   Jodi L. Jacobson, "Slavery (Yes, Slavery) Returns," *World • Watch*, (January/February 1992), Worldwatch Institute, Washington, D.C.

2.   Charles Taylor, *The Ethics of Authenticity* (Cambridge, MA: Harvard University Press, 1992), 78.

3.   Michael Kammen, *Spheres of Liberty, Changing Perceptions of Liberty in American Culture* (Madison, WI: University of Wisconsin Press, 1986), 11.

4.   Wilhelm F. von Humboldt, *The Limits of State Action*, ed. J. W. Burrow (London: Cambridge University Press, 1969), 9.

5.   Ibid., 9.

6.   Ibid., 9.

7.   Philippa Strum, *Louis D. Brandeis: Justice for the People* (New York: Schocken Books, Inc., 1984), 339-340 and Philippa Strum, *Brandeis: Beyond Progressivism* (Lawrence, Kansas: University Press of Kansas, 1993), 4 and Chapter 4.

8.   Louis D. Brandeis, *The Curse of Bigness: Miscellaneous Papers of Louis D. Brandeis*, ed. O. K. Fraenkel (Port Washington, NY: Kennikat Press, Inc., 1965), 188. See *Liggett Co. v. Lee* 288 U.S. 517 (1933).

9.   Phillip I. Blumberg, *The Multinational Challenge to Corporation Law: The Search for a New Corporate Personality* (New York: Oxford University Press, 1993).

10.   Ravi Batra, *The Myth of Free Trade, A Plan for America's Economic Revival* (New York: Charles Scribner's Sons, 1993), 193.

11.   E. F. Schumacher, *Small Is Beautiful: Economics As If People Mattered* (New York: Harper & Row, 1973), 267. See also Max Frenkel, "The Communal Basis of Swiss Liberty," *Publius: The Journal of Federalism*, 23 (Spring 1993), 61-70 where Swiss federalism prefers "small-scale" organizations.

12.   Schumacher, *Small Is Beautiful*, 317. Douglass C. North, a Nobel Prize winner, asks why economies diverge, what conditions lead to

divergence and how can we explain radically different performances over long periods of time? These questions must be posed to downsizing giant corporations who now reject the freedom to enterprise without limit under some conditions—namely peace, by downsizing. Douglass C. North, *Institutions, Institutional Change and Economic Performance* (Cambridge: Cambridge University Press, 1990). The answer may lie partly in the dissolution of part of the industrial-military complex that President Dwight Eisenhower in his farewell address to the Nation on January 17, 1960 warned America against. Monopoly and monopsony joined together in that economic complex that is now slowly unwinding. Robert Sobel, *The Age of Giant Corporations* (Westport, CT: Greenwood Press, 1984) Second Edition, 185-186.

Recent valuable additions to these debates make the subject lively and certainly more interesting than ever before. Coming to my attention too late to weave into the body and other parts of this book and noted here for reference are these exciting and illuminating works:

Brzezinski, Zbigniew. *Out of Control: Global Turmoil on the Eve of the Twenty-First Century.* New York: Collier Books, 1993.

Chomsky, Noam. *World Orders Old and New.* New York: Columbia University Press, 1994.

Goldsmith, Sir James. *The Trap.* New York: Carroll and Graf Publishers, Inc., 1994.

Harrison, Bennett. *Lean and Mean: The Changing Landscape of Corporate Power in the Age of Flexibility.* New York: BasicBooks, 1994.

Luttwak, Edward N. *The Endangered American Dream: How to Stop the United States from Becoming a Third-World Country and How to Win the Geo-Economic Struggle for Industrial Supremacy.* New York: Touchstone, 1994.

Miller, Lynn H. *Global Order: Values and Power in International Politics.* Boulder, CO: Westview Press, 1994. Third Edition.

Newman, Katherine S. *Declining Fortunes: The Withering of the American Dream.* New York: BasicBooks, 1993.

Phillips, Kevin. *Arrogant Capital: Washington, Wall Street, and the Frustration of American Politics.* Boston: Little, Brown and Company, 1994.

Shuman, Michael. *Towards a Global Village: International Community Development Initiatives.* London: Pluto Press, 1994.

Strobel, Frederick R. *Upward Dreams, Downward Mobility: The Economic Decline of the American Middle Class.* Lanham, MD: Rowman & Littlefield Publishers, Inc., 1993.

Stopford, John M., Susan Strange and John S. Henley. *Rival States, Rival Firms: Competition for World Market Shares.* Cambridge: Cambridge University Press, 1991.

Bibliography

Adler, Mortimer J. *The Idea of Freedom.* Garden City, NJ: Doubleday and Co., Vol. 1 1958, Vol. 2 1961.

Arendt, Hannah. *The Origins of Totalitarianism.* San Diego, CA: Harcourt Brace Jovanovich, Publishers, 1951.

Arkes, Hadley. *Beyond the Constitution.* Princeton, NJ: Princeton University Press, 1990.

Axelrod, Donald. *Shadow Government: The Hidden World of Public Authorities and How They Control Over $1 Trillion of Your Money.* New York: John Wiley & Sons, Inc., 1992.

Barber, Benjamin R. *The Aristocracy of Everyone: The Politics of Education and the Future of America.* New York: Ballantine Books, 1992.

Barnet, Richard J., and Ronald E. Müller. *Global Reach, The Power of the Multinational Corporations.* New York: Simon & Schuster, 1974.

Barth, Alan. *The Loyalty of Free Men.* New York: Viking Press, 1951.

_____. *The Price of Liberty.* New York: Viking Press, 1961.

_____. *The Rights of Free Men: An Essential Guide to Civil Liberties.* Edited by James E. Clayton. New York: Alfred A. Knopf, 1984.

Bartlett, Donald L., and James B. Steele. *America: What Went Wrong?* Kansas City, MO: Andrews and McNeel, 1992.

Barzun, Jacques. *The Culture We Deserve*. Middletown, CT: Wesleyan University Press, 1989.

Basler, Roy A., ed., *Collected Works of Abraham Lincoln*, Vol. 3. New Brunswick, NJ: Rutgers University Press, 1953.

Batra, Ravi. *The Myth of Free Trade, A Plan for American Economic Revival*. New York: Charles Scribner's Sons, 1993.

Beer, Samuel H. *To Make a Nation: The Rediscovery of American Federalism*. Cambridge, MA: Belknap Press of Harvard University, 1993.

Berlin, Isaiah. *Four Essays on Liberty*. London: Oxford University Press, 1969.

Berman, Harold J. *Law and Revolution: The Formation of Western Legal Tradition*. Cambridge, MA: Harvard University Press, 1983.

Blumberg, Phillip I. *The Multinational Challenge to Corporation Law: The Search for a New Corporate Personality*. New York: Oxford University Press, 1993.

Bodin, Jean. *On Sovereignty*. Edited and translated by J. H. Franklin. Cambridge: Cambridge University Press, 1992.

Bok, Derek. *The Cost of Talent: How Executives and Professionals Are Paid and How It Affects America*. New York: Free Press, 1993.

Brandeis, Louis D. *The Curse of Bigness: Miscellaneous Papers of Louis D. Brandeis*. Edited by O. K. Fraenkel. Port Washington, NY: Kennikat Press, Inc., 1965.

Burns, James MacGregor. *The Vineyard of Liberty*. New York: Alfred A. Knopf, 1982.

_____. *The Workshop of Democracy*. New York: Alfred A. Knopf, 1985.

_____. *The Crosswinds of Freedom*. New York: Alfred A. Knopf, 1989.

Camilleri, Joseph A., and Jim Falk. *The End of Sovereignty? The Politics of a Shrinking and Fragmenting World*. Hampshire County, England: Edward Elgar Publishing, Ltd., 1992.

Camus, Albert. *Resistance, Rebellion and Death*. Translated by Justin O'Brien. New York: Alfred A. Knopf, 1961.

Carnois, Bernard. *The Coherence of Kant's Doctrine of Freedom*. Chicago: University of Chicago Press, 1987.

Carson, Clayborne, et al., eds. *The Eyes on the Prize Civil Rights Reader: Documents, Speeches and Firsthand Accounts from the Black Freedom Struggle, 1954-1990*. New York: Penguin Books, 1991.

Chirot, Daniel. *Modern Tyrants: The Power and Prevalence of Evil in Our Age*. New York: Free Press, 1994.

Claude, Richard P., and Burns H. Weston (Editors). *Human Rights in the World Community*. (Second Edition). Philadelphia: University of Pennsylvania Press, 1992.

Clinard, Marshall B. *Corporate Corruption: The Abuse of Power*. New York: Praeger, 1990.

Clinard, Marshall B., and Peter C. Yeager. *Corporate Crime*. New York: The Free Press, 1980.

Clinton, Bill and Al Gore. *Putting People First: How We Can All Change America*. New York: Times Books, 1992.

Constant, Benjamin. *Political Writings*. Translated and edited by B. Fontana. Cambridge: Cambridge University Press, 1988.

Corwin, Edward S. *The Higher Law Background of American Constitutional Law*. Ithaca, NY: Cornell University Press, 1929.

Crystal, Graef S. *In Search of Excess: The Overcompensation of American Executives*. New York: W. W. Norton & Co., 1991.

Current, Richard N. *The Political Thought of Abraham Lincoln*. New York: Macmillan Publishing Co., 1967.

De Grazia, Edward. *Girls Lean Back Everywhere, the Laws of Obscenity and the Assault on Genius*. New York: Random House 1992.

Donohue, William A. *The Politics of the American Civil Liberties Union*. New Brunswick, NJ: Transaction Publishers, 1985.

_____. *The New Freedom*. New Brunswick, NJ: Transaction Publishers, 1990.

Edgerton, Robert B. *Sick Societies: Challenging the Myth of Primitive Harmony*. New York: Free Press, 1992.

Edsall, Thomas B. "Issue Has Aroused the Left," *Washington Post* 1 (November 8, 1993): 10-11.

Ehrenberg, Victor. *Man, State and Deity: Essays in Ancient History*. London: Methuen & Co., Ltd., 1974.

Elder, David A. *The Law of Privacy*. Deerfield, IL: Clark, Boardman and Callaghan, 1991.

Etzioni, Amitai. *The Spirit of Community*. New York: Crown Publishers, Inc., 1993.

Farrar, Cynthia. *The Origins of Democratic Thinking: The Invention of Politics in Classical Athens*. Cambridge: Cambridge University Press, 1988.

Frenkel, Max. "The Communal Basis of Swiss Liberty." *Publius: The Journal of Federalism* 23 (Spring 1993): 61-70.

Fuchs, Lawrence. *The American Kaleidoscope: Race, Ethnicity, and Civic Culture*. Hanover, NH: Wesleyan University Press, 1990.

Glasser, Ira. *Visions of Liberty: The Bill of Rights for All Americans*. New York: Arcade Publishing, 1991.

Greider, William. *Who Will Tell The People: The Betrayal of American Democracy*. New York: Simon & Schuster, 1992.

Gunther, Gerald. *Learned Hand, the Man and the Judge*. New York: Alfred A. Knopf, 1994.

Halpern, Stephen C. *The Future of Our Liberties*. Westport, CT: Greenwood Press, 1982.

Hand, Learned. 2d ed., enlarged. *The Spirit of Liberty*. New York: Alfred A. Knopf, 1953. Irving Dillard collection and edition.

Hargrove, John L., and Louis Henkin (Editors). *Human Rights: An Agenda for the Next Century*. Washington, DC: The American Society of International Law, 1994.

Hayek, Friedrich A. *The Constitution of Liberty*. Chicago: University of Chicago Press, 1960.

Hays, Steven W., and Cole B. Graham, Jr. *Handbook of Court Administration and Management*. New York: Marcel Dekker, Inc., 1993.

Heilbroner, Robert. *21st Century Capitalism*. New York: W. W. Norton & Co., 1993.

Heilbroner, Robert and Lester Thurow. *Economics Explained*. New York: Simon & Schuster, 1994.

Henkin, Louis, and John L. Hargrove (Editors). *Human Rights: An Agenda for the Next Century*. Washington, DC: The American Society of International Law, 1994.

Hentoff, Nat. *Free Speech for Me, But Not for Thee: How the American Left and Right Relentlessly Sensor Each Other*. New York: Harper Collins, Publishers, 1992.

Hinsley, Francis H. *Sovereignty*. New York: Basic Books, Inc., 1966.

Hughes, Robert. *Culture of Complaint, The Fraying of America*. New York: Oxford University Press, 1993.

Humana, Charles. *World Human Rights Guide*. New York: Fact on File Publications, 1986.

Humboldt, Wilhelm F. von. Edited by J. W. Burrow. *The Limits of State Action*. London: Cambridge University Press, 1969.

Ignatieff, Michael. *Blood and Belonging: Journeys into the New Nationalism*. New York: Farrar, Straus and Giroux, 1993.

Jacobson, Jodi L. "Slavery (Yes, Slavery) Returns." *World • Watch* (January/February 1992). Washington, D.C.: Worldwatch Institute.

Josephson, Matthew. *The Robber Barons: The Great American Capitalists 1861-1901*. New York: Harcourt Brace and World, 1934.

Kagan, Donald. *Pericles of Athens and the Birth of Democracy*. New York: Free Press, 1991.

Kammen, Michael. *Spheres of Liberty: Changing Perceptions of Liberty in American Culture*. Madison, WI: University of Wisconsin Press, 1986.

_____. *Sovereignty and Liberty: Constitutional Discourse in American Culture*. Madison, WI: University of Wisconsin Press, 1988.

Kausikan, Bilahari. "Asia's Different Standard." *Foreign Policy* 92 (1993): 24-41.

Kittrie, Nicholas. *The Right To Be Different: Deviance and Enforced Therapy*. Baltimore: Penguin Books, 1971.

Lapham, Lewis H. *The Wish for Kings*. New York: Grove Press, 1993.

Larson, Erik. *The Naked Consumer: How Our Private Lives Become Public Commodities*. New York: Henry Holt and Co., 1992.

Lasch, Christopher. *The Culture of Narcissism: American Life in An Age of Diminished Expectations*. New York: W. W. Norton & Co., 1979.

Lewis, C. S. *Studies in Words*. London: Cambridge University Press, 1967.

Lippmann, Walter. *Liberty and the News*. New York: Harcourt, Brace and Howe, 1920.

MacKinnon, Catherine A. *Toward a Feminist Theory of the State*. Cambridge, MA: Harvard University Press, 1989.

Marcus, Mavea. *Truman and the Steel Seizure Case: The Limits of Presidential Power*. New York: Columbia University Press, 1977.

McCullough, David. *Truman*. New York: Simon & Schuster, 1992.

Merriam, Charles E. *History of the Theory of Sovereignty Since Rousseau*. 1900. Reprint, New York: AMS Press, Inc., 1968.

Mill, John Stuart. *On Liberty*. 1978 ed. Edited by E. Rapaport, 1978 ed. Indianapolis: Hackett Publishing Co., Inc., 1859.

Miller, David, ed. *Popper Selections*. Princeton, NJ: Princeton University Press, 1985.

Muller, Herbert Joseph. *The Loom of History*. New York: Harper, 1958.

_____. *The Issues of Freedom: Paradoxes and Promises*. New York: Harper, 1960.

_____. *Freedom in the Ancient World*. New York: Harper and Brothers, 1961.

_____. *Freedom in the Western World*. New York: Harper & Row, 1963.

_____. *Religion and Freedom in the Modern World*. Chicago: University of Chicago Press, 1963.

_____. *Freedom in the Modern World*. New York: Harper & Row, 1966.

Muller, Jerry Z. *Adam Smith in His Time and Ours, Designing the Decent Society*. New York: Free Press, 1993.

Murphy, Paul L. *World War I and the Origin of Civil Liberties in the United States*. New York: W. W. Norton & Co., 1979.

Nader, Ralph, Mark Green, and Joel Seligman. *Taming the Giant Corporation*. New York: W. W. Norton & Co., 1976.

Nader, Ralph, William Greider, et al. *The Case Against Free Trade: GATT, NAFTA and the Globalization of Corporate Power*. San Francisco: Earth Island Press, 1993.

Neely, Mark E., Jr. *The Fate of Liberty*. New York: Oxford University Press, 1991.

Neier, Aryeh. "Asia's Unacceptable Standard." *Foreign Policy* 92:42-51 (Fall, 1993).

North, Douglass C. *Institutions, Institutional Change and Economic Performance*. Cambridge: Cambridge University Press, 1990.

Ostwald, Martin. *From Popular Sovereignty to the Sovereignty of Law: Law, Society and Politics in Fifth-Century Athens*. Berkeley, CA: University of California Press, 1986.

Pagano, Michael A., and Ann O'M. Bowman. "The State of American Federalism 1992-93." *Publius, The Journal of Federalism* 23 (Summer 1993): 1-22

Patterson, Orlando. *Freedom.* Vol. I, *Freedom in the Making of Western Culture.* New York: Basic Books, 1991.

Phillips, Kevin. *The Politics of Rich and Poor: Wealth and the American Electorate in the Reagan Aftermath.* New York: Random House, 1990.

Pohlenz, Max. *Freedom in Greek Life and Thought: The History of An Ideal.* Dordrecht, Holland: D. Reidel Publishing, 1966.

Rhode, Deborah L. *Justice and Gender, Sex Discrimination and the Law.* Cambridge, MA: Harvard University Press, 1989.

Rivlin, Alice M. *Reviving The American Dream: The Economy, The States and The Federal Government.* Washington, DC: The Brookings Institution, 1992.

Saari, David J. "Separation of Powers, Judicial Impartiality and Judicial Independence: Primary Goals of Court Management Education." *Handbook of Court Administration and Management*, Chapter 7. New York: Marcel Dekker, Inc., 1993.

Saxonhouse, Arlene W. *Fear of Diversity, The Birth of Political Science in Ancient Greek Thought.* Chicago: University of Chicago Press, 1992.

Schlesinger, Arthur M., Jr. *The Disuniting of America.* New York: W. W. Norton & Co., 1992.

Schoenbrod, David. *Power Without Reponsibility, How Congress Abuses the People Through Delegation.* New Haven, CT: Yale University Press, 1993.

Schumacher, E. F. *Small Is Beautiful: Economics As If People Mattered.* New York: Harper & Row, 1973.

Shapiro, Joseph P. *No Pity: People with Disabilities Forging a New Civil Rights Movement.* New York: Times Books, 1993.

Shevardnadze, Eduard. *The Future Belongs to Freedom.* New York: Free Press, 1991.

Sobel, Robert. *The Age of Giant Corporations.* Second Edition. Westport, CT: Greenwood Press, 1984.

Speiser, Stuart M. *Lawyers and the American Dream.* New York: M. Evans & Co., 1993.

Spence, Gerry. *From Freedom to Slavery: The Rebirth of Tyranny in America.* New York: St. Martin's Press, 1993.

Steel, Ronald. *Walter Lippmann and the American Century.* Boston: Little, Brown & Co., 1980.

Strum, Philippa. *Louis D. Brandeis: Justice for the People.* New York: Schocken Books, Inc., 1984.

_____. *Brandeis: Beyond Progressivism.* Lawrence, Kansas: University Press of Kansas, 1993.

Styron, William. *Darkness Visible.* New York: Random House, 1990.

Sutherland, Edwin H. *White Collar Crime: The Uncut Version.* Dryden Press, 1949. New Haven, CT: Yale University Press, 1983.

Taylor, Charles. *The Ethics of Authenticity.* Cambridge, MA: Harvard University Press, 1992.

Taylor, Telford. *The Anatomy of the Nuremberg Trials.* New York: Alfred A. Knopf, 1992.

Teichgraeber, Richard F. *"Free Trade" and Moral Philosophy: Rethinking the Sources of Adam Smith's* Wealth of Nations. Durham, NC: Duke University Press, 1986.

Tolchin, Martin, and Susan J. Tolchin. *Selling Our Security: The Erosion of America's Assets.* New York: Alfred A. Knopf, 1992.

Truell, Peter, and Larry Gurwin. *False Profits: The Inside Story of BCCI, The World's Most Corrupt Financial Empire.* Boston: Houghton Mifflin Co., 1992.

United Nations. *World Conference on Human Rights, the Vienna Declaration and Programme of Action,* 1993.

United Nations Development Programme (UNDP). *Human Development Report 1991*. New York: Oxford University Press, 1991.

United States Advisory Commission on Intergovernmental Relations. *A Commission Report, Federal Statutory Preemption of State and Local Authority: History, Inventory and Issues*. Washington, D.C., September 1992.

_____. *Federal Regulation of State and Local Governments: The Mixed Record of the 1980's*. Washington, D.C., July 1993.

Vanderbilt, Arthur T. *The Doctrine of the Separation of Powers and Its Present Day Significance*. Lincoln, NE: University of Nebraska Press, 1953.

Walker, Samuel. *In Defense of American Liberties: A History of the ACLU*. New York: Oxford University Press, 1990.

Weston, Burns H., and Richard P. Claude (Editors). *Human Rights in the World Community*. (Second Edition). Philadelphia: University of Pennsylvania Press, 1992.

Williams, Bernard. *Shame and Necessity*. Berkeley: University of California Press, 1993.

Wolf, Naomi. *Fire with Fire: The New Female Power and How It Will Change the 21st Century*. New York: Random House, 1993.

Wriston, Walter B. *The Twilight of Sovereignty: How the Information Revolution Is Transforming Our World*. New York: Charles Scribner's Sons, 1992.

Zimmerman, Joseph F. *Federal Preemption, the Silent Revolution*. Ames, Iowa: Iowa State University Press, 1991.

Author and Proper Name Index

Adler, Mortimer J., xi, xiii, 28, 29, 38, 41, 52, 121, 141
Alfred ("the Great"), 46
Allen, Ronald, 86
Arendt, Hannah, 19, 142
Aristophanes 107
Arkes, Hadley, 115
Axelrod, Donald, 105

Baldwin, Roger, 21
Barnet, Richard J., 147
Barth, Alum, 22
Bartlett, Donald L., 91, 92
Barzun, Jacques, 49, 144, 145
Batra, Ravi, 124, 147, 150
Beer, Samuel H., 148, 149
Berle, Adolph, 124
Berlin, Isaiah, 41, 42, 52, 144
Berman, Harold J., 47, 48, 73, 144
Blackstone, William, 98
Blumberg, Phillip I., 150
Bodin, Jean, 147
Bok, Derek, 88, 146
Brandeis, Louis D. (Justice), 109, 123-125, 150
Brzezinski, Zbigniew, 151

Burns, James MacGregor, 64, 72, 73, 87, 145, 146
Burrow, J. W., 122
Bush, George H. W., 83
Byron, George Gordon (Lord), 50, 55

Camilleri, Joseph A., 147
Camus, Albert, xiv, 1, 76-81, 90, 123, 146
Casey, Robert P., 32
Chaucer, Geoffrey, 46
Chirot, Daniel, 148
Chomsky, Noam, 151
Cicero, Marcus Tullius, 46, 114
Claude, Richard P., 143
Clayton, James E., 22
Clinard, Marshall B., 91
Clinton, Bill, 15, 90, 142, 147
Commanger, Henry Steele, 38
Constant, Benjamin, 147
Corwin, Edward S., 150
Crandall, Robert, 86
Crystal, Graef S., 11, 88, 90, 94, 124, 146

De Grazia, Edward, 110
Debs, Eugene V., 22

Dennis, Eugene, 22
Donohue, William A., 9-11, 15, 21, 92, 142
Draper, William H., 28
DuPont, Lamont, 89, 90

Edgerton, Robert B., 141, 146
Edsall, Thomas B., 147
Ehrenberg, Victor, xiv, 50-52, 75, 96, 106, 107, 120, 144, 145, 148, 149
Einstein, Albert, 19
Eisenhower, Dwight D., 151
Elder, David A., 145
Etzioni, Amitai, 142

Falk, Jim, 147
Farrar, Cynthia, 49, 144
Finely, Karen, 1
Frenkel, Max, 149
Freud, Sigmund, 9
Friedman, Milton, 86
Fuchs, Lawrence, 100

Galbraith, John Kenneth, 67
Galileo (Astronomer), 109
Gideon, Clarence, 22
Glasser, Ira, 31, 143
Goering, Herman, 75
Goldsmith, Sir James, 151
Gore, Al, 15, 90, 142, 147
Grace, Eugene, 89, 90
Graham, Cole B., Jr., 148
Green, Mark, 91
Greider, William, 82, 84, 91, 92, 94, 124, 147
Gunther, Gerald, 146
Gurwin, Larry, 82

Halpern, Stephen C., 143
Hamilton, Alexander, 98
Hammer, Armand, 24
Hammurabi, 62

Hand, Learned (Judge), xiv, xv, 79-81, 90, 108, 109, 123, 146, 149
Hardwick, Michael, 22
Harrison, Bennett, 151
Hayek, Friedrich A., 64
Hays, Steven W., 148
Heilbroner, Robert, 145, 148
Henley, John S., 151
Henry, Patrick, 78
Hentoff, Nat, 99
Herder, Johann Gottfried von (Philosopher), 113
Hilary, Richard, 77
Hitler, Adolph, 76
Hobbes, Thomas, 17, 20
Homer (Poet), 107
Hughes, Robert, 148
Humana, Charles, 28, 42
Humboldt, Wilhelm F. von, 121-123, 150
Hume, David, 98
Hussein, Saddam, 102

Ignatieff, Michael, 146

Jackson, Robert H. (Justice), 108, 109
Jacobson, Jodi L., 150
Jefferson, Thomas, 94, 96, 98

Kagan, Donald, 107, 149
Kammen, Michael, xii, xiv, 57, 59, 60, 63-65, 73, 85, 87, 97, 98, 109, 110, 121, 141, 143, 144, 147-150
Kant, Immanuel, 41, 50, 59, 114
Kausikan, Bilahari, 143
Keitel, Wilhelm, 75
Kennedy, John F., 72
King, Rodney, 1, 24, 62
Kissinger, Henry, 93
Kittrie, Nicholas, 5

Lapham, Lewis H., 82-84, 146
Larson, Erik, 91
Lasch, Christopher, 72
Lewis, C. S., 45-48, 143, 144
Lincoln, Abraham, xii, 43-44, 60,
   63, 73, 90, 107, 119, 120
Lippmann, Walter, xiv, 60, 61,
   119, 146
Locke, John, 57, 97, 98
Luther, Martin, 109
Luttwak, Edward N., 151

MacKinnon, Catherine A., 142
Madison, James, xii, 31, 60, 93,
   98
Marcus, Mavea, 144
Marcuse, Herbert, 10
Marshall, Thurgood (Justice), 3
Marx, Karl, 66, 94
McCullough, David, 145
McReynolds, James Clark (Jus-
   tice), 111
Means, Gardner, 124
Mill, John Stuart, xv, 9, 13-15,
   19, 30, 36, 41, 57, 71, 84, 97,
   106, 109, 110, 114, 121-123,
   141-143, 149
Miller, Lynn H., 151
Miranda, Ernesto, 22
Montesquieu (Philosopher), 97,
   102
Moseley-Braun, Carol, 3
Muller, Herbert Joseph, 48,
   70-73, 144, 145, 148
Muller, Jerry Z., 147
Müller, Ronald E., 147
Murphy, Paul, L., 22, 143

Nader, Ralph, 31, 91, 147
Neely, Mark E., Jr., 43, 44, 144
Neier, Aryeh, 43
Newman, Katherine S., 151
Nin, Anaïs, 2

Nixon, Richard, 93
North, Douglass C., 151

Ostwald, Martin, 148

Parks, Rosa, 22
Patterson, Orlando, xi-xiii, 29,
   38, 48, 52, 55, 73, 77, 93, 121,
   141
Pericles, 48, 49, 55, 60, 107
Perot, Ross, 24, 83
Phillips, Kevin, 143, 151
Plato, 111
Plessy, Homer A., 23
Pohlenz, Max, 49, 144
Popper, Karl, 19, 41, 53, 142, 144

Reich, Charles, 10
Rhode, Deborah L., 142
Rivlin, Alice M., 91, 92, 103
Robinson, Harvey, 108
Rockefeller, Jay, 24
Roe, Jane, 22, 30
Roosevelt, Franklin D., 60, 72
Rousseau, Jean Jacques, 97

Saari, David J., 148
Saxonhouse, Arlene W., 148
Schlesinger, Arthur M., Jr., 100,
   101, 148
Schopenhauer, Arthur, 2
Schumacher, E. F., 125, 150
Scott, Dred, 22
Seligman, Joel, 91
Shakespeare, William, xiv
Shapiro, Joseph P., 142
Shevardnaze, Eduard, 78
Shultz, George, 93
Shuman, Michael, 151
Slater, Philip, 10
Smith, Adam, 147, 148
Sobel, Robert, 151
Socrates (Philosopher), 96, 107

Sophocles (Dramatist), 56
Spafford, Horatio G., 94
Sparta, 111
Speiser, Stuart M., 141
Spence, Gerry, 82, 84, 146
Steele, James B., 91, 92
Stopford, John M., 151
Strange, Susan, 151
Strobel, Frederick R., 151
Strum, Philippa, 123, 150
Styron, William, 76, 146
Sutherland, Edwin H., 89, 146

Taylor, Charles, 16, 38, 73,
    113-115, 120, 142, 149, 150
Taylor, Telford, 146
Teichgraeber, Richard F., 148
Thucydides (Historian), 107
Thurow, Lester, 145, 148
Tolchin, Martin and Susan, 70,
    93, 99, 145, 147

Truell, Peter, 82
Truman, Harry S., 64, 144

Vanderbilt, Arthur T., 103, 148
Victoria (Queen), 13
Vyshinsky, Andrei, 103

Walker, Samuel, 21, 14
Weston, Burns H., 143
Wilder (Governor, VA), 3
Williams, Bernard, 149
Winthrop, John, xii, 98
Wolf, Naomi, 142
Wolf, Stephen, 86
Wriston, Walter B., 93-95, 148

Yeager, Peter C., 91
Yourcenar, Margaret, 48

Zimmerman, Joseph F., 162

Subject Index

American Dream of Freedom:
defined, xii, 99-102; dissent
from, 81-85
American Freedom Issues:
abortion, 31-37, 38, 57; AIDS,
1-3; basic contradictions, 7,
26; bastardizing trends, 10;
children, 3, 4; disabled
people, 10; drugs, 5, 6;
homosexuality, 110, 111;
mentally ill, 4, 5; minority
rights, 3, 4; pornography,
110, 111; solutions, 12, 13; too
little freedom, 17-25; too
much freedom, 9-16
Ancient Greek origins of liberty,
48-50, 78, 80, 96, 106, 107,
133-140
Architecture of freedom, 53-55
Authenticity and inner liberty,
113, 114
Authority and freedom, 63

Book plan, xiii

Civic liberty. *See* Freedom, new
paradigm
Civil liberties logic, 20-23, 31-37

Congress, United States,
constitutional limits of
power, 111-113
Conscience and liberty, 106
Constitutional order, limits to
115, 116, 121-123

Drug searches and seizures, 5, 6

E pluribus unum, 3, 99-102
Equality and freedom, 64, 65,
110

Federalism. *See* Governments
Feudalism, modern aspects, 92,
93
Fortune 500 corporations. *See*
Giant corporations and free
enterprise
Free enterprise. *See* Giant
corporations and free
enterprise
Freedom and contingency:
persistent issues, 60-63, 67,
69; sense of contingency, 60-
63
Freedom and property, 64

Freedom, historical perspectives
    of:
    conservative, 9, 19
    different approaches: Burns,
        72-74; dictionaries, 44-48;
        Lincoln type, 43, 44;
        Muller, 70-72; United
        Nations, 42, 43
    liberal, 17-25
Freedom, new paradigm:
    civic liberty, 52, 56, 95-97;
        applied, 74, 95-102, 117,
        118; defined, 58, 95-102
    inner liberty, 52, 56, 57;
        applied, 74, 106-116, 117,
        118; defined, 58-60
    national freedom: analytical
        questions, 117-119;
        applied, 74-95; Camus, 76-
        79; defined, 48-51, 55, 56;
        giant corporate impact on,
        74-95; Hand, 79-81

General agreement on trades
    and tariffs (GATT), 93, 124
Geophysical freedom, 17-19
Giant corporations and free
    enterprise, 24, 123-125;
    corporate sovereignty, 86-94;
    executive pay, 11, 88, 90;
    international trade and
    technology, 70, 86, 93-95;
    loyalty and betrayal issues,
    85, 92; Mannonism, 88;
    treason, 89; white collar
    crime and corruption, 81-94
Governments: federalism, 38,
    98, 102-105; gridlock, 102,
    103; limits on Congress, 111-
    113; limits on states, 121-123;
    preemption, 104, 105;
    separation of powers, 38, 98,
    102-105; shadow govern-

ments, 11, 12, 105, 106;
    suppression of liberty, 23-25;
    term limits, 12

Human rights. See United
    Nations; 127-128

Individualism, 15, 16
Inner liberty. See Freedom, new
    paradigm
International issues of freedom.
    See Freedom, new paradigm;
    United Nations
Issues of freedom:
    hierarchy of values, xiii-xix
    sovereignty: corporate, 86;
        popular, 95; state, 87, 88
    state role (See freedom, new
        paradigm)

Justice and freedom, 65, 75, 76,
    91, 110

Liberty. See Freedom, new
    paradigm

Melting pot, 99-102
Monkeying around, 108-113
Moral horizon, 115, 116
Multinational corporations. See
    Giant corporations

National liberty. See Freedom,
    new paradigm
Nationalism, 74
North American Free Trade
    Agreement (NAFTA), 93
Nuremberg War Crime Trials,
    75, 76

Open society, 101

Parental responsibility:
    contemporary concerns, 15,
    16; historical issues, 13-15
Privacy and freedom, 4, 65, 66,
    104. *See also* American
    Freedom Issues, abortion

Religions and liberty, 109
Responsibility, 63

Separation of powers. *See*
    Governments
Slavery, 10, 67, 119, 120
Supreme Court of the United
    States, decisional role in
    liberty, 31-37

Technology impact, 93-95
Tyranny, modern effects, 102,
    112

United Nations: human
    development, 28-30, 42, 43;
    universal declaration of
    human rights, 29, 107;
    universality of human rights,
    29; Vienna Declaration and
    Conference, 29, 107

About the Author

DAVID J. SAARI is Professor of Public Affairs at the American University in Washington, D.C. He holds a B.A. and J.D. from the University of Minnesota and is the author of *American Court Management* (Quorum Books, 1982) and *The Court and Free-Lance Reporter Profession* (Quorum Books, 1988).

www.ingramcontent.com/pod-product-compliance
Lightning Source LLC
Chambersburg PA
CBHW062030270326
41929CB00014B/2391